Wonderful ways to prepare

SALADS

by JO ANN SHIRLEY

Printed in Canada

Wonderful ways to prepare

SALADS

PLAYMORE INC NEW YORK USA
UNDER ARRANGEMENT WITH
I. WALDMAN & SON INC

AYERS & JAMES PTY LTD
CROWS NEST AUSTRALIA

STAFFORD PEMBERTON PUBLISHING
KNUTSFORD UNITED KINGDOM

FIRST PUBLISHED 1978

PUBLISHED IN THE USA
BY PLAYMORE INC.
UNDER ARRANGEMENT WITH I. WALDMAN & SON INC.

PUBLISHED IN AUSTRALIA
BY AYERS & JAMES PTY. LTD.
CROWS NEST.   AUSTRALIA

PUBLISHED IN THE UNITED KINGDOM
BY STAFFORD PEMBERTON PUBLISHING
KNUTSFORD CHESIRE

ISBN 0 86908 059 8

OVEN TEMPERATURE GUIDE

Description	Gas		Electric		Mark
	C	F	C	F	
Cool	100	200	110	225	¼
Very Slow	120	250	120	250	½
Slow	150	300	150	300	1-2
Moderately slow	160	325	170	340	3
Moderate	180	350	200	400	4
Moderately hot	190	375	220	425	5-6
Hot	200	400	230	450	6-7
Very hot	230	450	250	475	8-9

LIQUID MEASURES

IMPERIAL	METRIC
1 teaspoon	5 ml
1 tablespoon	20 ml
2 fluid ounces (¼ cup)	62.5 ml
4 fluid ounces (½ cup)	125 ml
8 fluid ounces (1 cup)	250 ml
1 pint (16 ounces — 2 cups)*	500 ml

* (The imperial pint is equal to 20 fluid ounces.)

SOLID MEASURES

AVOIRDUPOIS	METRIC
1 ounce	30 g
4 ounces (¼ lb)	125 g
8 ounces (½ lb)	250 g
12 ounces (¾ lb)	375 g
16 ounces (1 lb)	500 g
24 ounces (1½ lb)	750 g
32 ounces (2 lb)	1000 g (1 kg)

CUP AND SPOON REPLACEMENTS FOR OUNCES

INGREDIENT	½ oz	1 oz	2 oz	3 oz	4 oz	5 oz	6 oz	7 oz	8 oz
Almonds, ground	2 T	¼ C	½ C	¾ C	1¼ C	1⅓ C	1⅔ C	2 C	2¼ C
slivered	6 t	¼ C	½ C	¾ C	1 C	1⅓ C	1⅔ C	2 C	2¼ C
whole	2 T	¼ C	⅓ C	½ C	¾ C	1 C	1¼ C	1⅓ C	1½ C
Apples, dried whole	3 T	½ C	1 C	1⅓ C	2 C	2⅓ C	2¾ C	3⅓ C	3¾ C
Apricots, chopped	2 T	¼ C	½ C	¾ C	1 C	1¼ C	1½ C	1¾ C	2 C
whole	2 T	3 T	½ C	⅔ C	1 C	1¼ C	1⅓ C	1½ C	1¾ C
Arrowroot	1 T	2 T	⅓ C	½ C	⅔ C	¾ C	1 C	1¼ C	1⅓ C
Baking Powder	1 T	2 T	⅓ C	½ C	⅔ C	¾ C	1 C	1 C	1¼ C
Baking Soda	1 T	2 T	⅓ C	½ C	⅔ C	¾ C	1 C	1 C	1¼ C
Barley	1 T	2 T	¼ C	½ C	⅔ C	¾ C	1 C	1 C	1¼ C
Breadcrumbs, dry	2 T	¼ C	½ C	¾ C	1 C	1¼ C	1½ C	1¾ C	2 C
soft	¼ C	½ C	1 C	1½ C	2 C	2½ C	3 C	3⅔ C	4¼ C
Biscuit Crumbs	2 T	¼ C	½ C	¾ C	1¼ C	1⅓ C	1⅔ C	2 C	2¼ C
Butter	3 t	6 t	¼ C	⅓ C	½ C	⅔ C	¾ C	1 C	1 C
Cheese, grated, lightly packed,									
natural cheddar	6 t	¼ C	½ C	¾ C	1 C	1¼ C	1½ C	1¾ C	2 C
Processed cheddar	5 t	2 T	⅓ C	⅔ C	¾ C	1 C	1¼ C	1½ C	1⅔ C
Parmesan, Romano	6 t	¼ C	½ C	¾ C	1 C	1⅓ C	1⅔ C	2 C	2¼ C
Cherries, candied, chopped	1 T	2 T	⅓ C	½ C	¾ C	1 C	1 C	1⅓ C	1½ C
whole	1 T	2 T	⅓ C	½ C	⅔ C	¾ C	1 C	1¼ C	1⅓ C
Cocoa	2 T	¼ C	½ C	¾ C	1¼ C	1⅓ C	1⅔ C	2 C	2¼ C
Coconut, desiccated	2 T	⅓ C	⅔ C	1 C	1⅓ C	1⅔ C	2 C	2⅓ C	2⅔ C
shredded	⅓ C	⅔ C	1¼ C	1¾ C	2½ C	3 C	3⅔ C	4⅓ C	5 C
Cornstarch	6 t	3 T	½ C	⅔ C	1 C	1¼ C	1½ C	1⅔ C	2 C
Corn Syrup	2 t	1 T	2 T	¼ C	⅓ C	½ C	½ C	⅔ C	⅔ C
Coffee, ground	2 T	⅓ C	⅔ C	1 C	1⅓ C	1⅔ C	2 C	2⅓ C	2⅔ C
instant	3 T	½ C	1 C	1⅓ C	1¾ C	2¼ C	2⅔ C	3 C	3½ C
Cornflakes	½ C	1 C	2 C	3 C	4¼ C	5¼ C	6¼ C	7⅓ C	8⅓ C
Cream of Tartar	1 T	2 T	⅓ C	½ C	⅔ C	¾ C	1 C	1 C	1¼ C
Currants	1 T	2 T	⅓ C	⅔ C	¾ C	1 C	1¼ C	1½ C	1⅔ C
Custard Powder	6 t	3 T	½ C	⅔ C	1 C	1¼ C	1½ C	1⅔ C	2 C
Dates, chopped	1 T	2 T	⅓ C	⅔ C	¾ C	1 C	1¼ C	1½ C	1⅔ C
whole, pitted	1 T	2 T	⅓ C	½ C	¾ C	1 C	1¼ C	1⅓ C	1½ C
Figs, chopped	1 T	2 T	⅓ C	½ C	¾ C	1 C	1 C	1⅓ C	1½ C
Flour, all-purpose or cake	6 t	¼ C	½ C	¾ C	1 C	1¼ C	1½ C	1¾ C	2 C
wholemeal	6 t	3 T	½ C	⅔ C	1 C	1¼ C	1⅓ C	1⅔ C	1¾ C
Fruit, mixed	1 T	2 T	⅓ C	½ C	¾ C	1 C	1¼ C	1⅓ C	1½ C
Gelatine	5 t	2 T	⅓ C	½ C	¾ C	1 C	1 C	1¼ C	1½ C
Ginger, crystallised pieces	1 T	2 T	⅓ C	½ C	¾ C	1 C	1¼ C	1⅓ C	1½ C
ground	6 t	⅓ C	½ C	¾ C	1¼ C	1½ C	1¾ C	2 C	2¼ C
preserved, heavy syrup	1 T	2 T	⅓ C	½ C	⅔ C	¾ C	1 C	1 C	1¼ C
Glucose, liquid	2 t	1 T	2 T	¼ C	⅓ C	½ C	½ C	⅔ C	⅔ C
Haricot Beans	1 T	2 T	⅓ C	½ C	⅔ C	¾ C	1 C	1 C	1¼ C

In this table, t represents teaspoonful, T represents tablespoonful and C represents cupful.

CUP AND SPOON REPLACEMENTS FOR OUNCES (Cont.)

INGREDIENT	½ oz	1 oz	2 oz	3 oz	4 oz	5 oz	6 oz	7 oz	8 oz
Honey	2 t	1 T	2 T	¼ C	⅓ C	½ C	½ C	⅔ C	⅔ C
Jam	2 t	1 T	2 T	¼ C	⅓ C	½ C	½ C	⅔ C	¾ C
Lentils	1 T	2 T	⅓ C	½ C	⅔ C	¾ C	1 C	1 C	1¼ C
Macaroni (see pasta)									
Milk Powder, full cream	2 T	¼ C	½ C	¾ C	1¼ C	1⅓ C	1⅔ C	2 C	2¼ C
non fat	2 T	⅓ C	¾ C	1¼ C	1½ C	2 C	2⅓ C	2¾ C	3¼ C
Nutmeg	6 t	3 T	½ C	⅔ C	¾ C	1 C	1¼ C	1½ C	1⅔ C
Nuts, chopped	6 t	¼ C	½ C	¾ C	1 C	1¼ C	1½ C	1¾ C	2 C
Oatmeal	1 T	2 T	½ C	⅔ C	¾ C	1 C	1¼ C	1½ C	1⅔ C
Olives, whole	1 T	2 T	⅓ C	⅔ C	¾ C	1 C	1¼ C	1½ C	1⅔ C
sliced	1 T	2 T	⅓ C	⅔ C	¾ C	1 C	1¼ C	1½ C	1⅔ C
Pasta, short (e.g. macaroni)	1 T	2 T	⅓ C	⅔ C	¾ C	1 C	1¼ C	1½ C	1⅔ C
Peaches, dried & whole	1 T	2 T	⅓ C	⅔ C	¾ C	1 C	1¼ C	1½ C	1⅔ C
chopped	6 t	¼ C	½ C	¾ C	1 C	1¼ C	1½ C	1¾ C	2 C
Peanuts, shelled, raw, whole	1 T	2 T	⅓ C	½ C	¾ C	1 C	1¼ C	1⅓ C	1½ C
roasted	1 T	2 T	⅓ C	⅔ C	¾ C	1 C	1¼ C	1½ C	1⅔ C
Peanut Butter	3 t	6 t	3 T	⅓ C	½ C	½ C	⅔ C	¾ C	1 C
Peas, split	1 T	2 T	⅓ C	½ C	⅔ C	¾ C	1 C	1 C	1¼ C
Peel, mixed	1 T	2 T	⅓ C	½ C	¾ C	1 C	1 C	1¼ C	1½ C
Potato, powder	1 T	2 T	¼ C	⅓ C	½ C	⅔ C	¾ C	1 C	1¼ C
flakes	¼ C	½ C	1 C	1⅓ C	2 C	2⅓ C	2¾ C	3⅓ C	3¾ C
Prunes, chopped	1 T	2 T	⅓ C	½ C	⅔ C	¾ C	1 C	1¼ C	1⅓ C
whole pitted	1 T	2 T	⅓ C	½ C	⅔ C	¾ C	1 C	1 C	1¼ C
Raisins	2 T	¼ C	⅓ C	½ C	¾ C	1 C	1 C	1⅓ C	1½ C
Rice, short grain, raw	1 T	2 T	¼ C	½ C	⅔ C	¾ C	1 C	1 C	1¼ C
long grain, raw	1 T	2 T	⅓ C	½ C	¾ C	1 C	1¼ C	1⅓ C	1½ C
Rice Bubbles	⅔ C	1¼ C	2½ C	3⅔ C	5 C	6¼ C	7½ C	8¾ C	10 C
Rolled Oats	2 T	⅓ C	⅔ C	1 C	1⅓ C	1¾ C	2 C	2½ C	2¾ C
Sago	2 T	¼ C	⅓ C	½ C	¾ C	1 C	1 C	1¼ C	1½ C
Salt, common	3 t	6 t	¼ C	⅓ C	½ C	⅔ C	¾ C	1 C	1 C
Semolina	1 T	2 T	⅓ C	½ C	¾ C	1 C	1 C	1⅓ C	1½ C
Spices	6 t	3 T	¼ C	⅓ C	½ C	½ C	⅔ C	¾ C	1 C
Sugar, plain	3 t	6 t	¼ C	⅓ C	½ C	⅔ C	¾ C	1 C	1 C
confectioners'	1 T	2 T	⅓ C	½ C	¾ C	1 C	1 C	1¼ C	1½ C
moist brown	1 T	2 T	⅓ C	½ C	¾ C	1 C	1 C	1⅓ C	1½ C
Tapioca	1 T	2 T	⅓ C	½ C	⅔ C	¾ C	1 C	1¼ C	1⅓ C
Treacle	2 t	1 T	2 T	¼ C	⅓ C	½ C	½ C	⅔ C	⅔ C
Walnuts, chopped	2 T	¼ C	½ C	¾ C	1 C	1¼ C	1½ C	1¾ C	2 C
halved	2 T	⅓ C	⅔ C	1 C	1¼ C	1½ C	1¾ C	2¼ C	2½ C
Yeast, dried	6 t	3 T	½ C	⅔ C	1 C	1¼ C	1⅓ C	1⅔ C	1¾ C
compressed	3 t	6 t	3 T	⅓ C	½ C	½ C	⅔ C	¾ C	1 C

In this table, t represents teaspoonful, T represents tablespoonful and C represents cupful.

Contents

Salads

Russian Salad

¼ lb (125 g) ham, diced
¼ lb (125 g) shrimp,
   cooked and chopped
1 small can tuna fish
1 tablespoon capers
1 hard-boiled egg, riced
6 olives, pitted
6 anchovy fillets
Russian Dressing (see index)

1 small cauliflower, boiled
   for five minutes
   and cut into flowerets
1 cup peas, cooked
2 carrots, sliced
2 potatoes, cooked and diced
½ cup cooked beets
   chopped
2 tomatoes, sliced

1. Put layers of vegetables, ham, shrimp and tuna fish in a salad bowl. Cover each layer with Russian Dressing.
2. Garnish with riced egg, olives and anchovy fillets.

Serves 6-8.

Shrimp Salad

2 tablespoons mayonnaise
3 tablespoons (60 g) cream
 cheese
1 tablespoon prepared
 horseradish sauce
2 tablespoons cream
1 green pepper, finely chopped

2 tablespoons chopped parsley
2 stalks celery, chopped
1 lb (500 g) cooked peeled
 shrimp
lettuce
lemon, cut in wedges

1. Mix the mayonnaise with the cream cheese, horseradish sauce, cream, pepper and parsley. Blend thoroughly.
2. Combine the celery and the shrimp.
3. Pour the dressing over the shrimp and mix well.
4. Arrange lettuce leaves in a bowl and spoon the salad on top.
5. Garnish with lemon wedges.

Serves 6.

Red Cabbage Salad

½ red cabbage
2 green apples
2 onions, chopped
½ green pepper, sliced
2 hard-boiled eggs,
 quartered
French Dressing or Sour
 Cream Dressing (see index)

1. Shred the cabbage finely.
2. Core (but do not peel) and slice the apples.
3. Add the cabbage to the apples, onions and green pepper and mix well.
4. Pour French Dressing or Sour Cream Dressing over the salad and toss thoroughly.
5. Garnish with quartered eggs.

Serves 4-6.

Tomato and Macaroni Salad

1 cup (150 g) macaroni
1 lb (500 g) tomatoes
2 tablespoons prepared
    horseradish sauce
½ cup (125 ml) cream
¼ cup (62.5 g) sour cream
salt
1 tablespoon vinegar
parsley to garnish

1. Cook the macaroni in boiling water until just tender. Drain and cool.
2. Cut the tomatoes into small pieces and mix with the macaroni.
3. Blend together the horseradish sauce, cream, sour cream, salt and vinegar.
4. Pour over the macaroni and tomatoes and mix thoroughly.
5. Garnish with parsley.

Serves 6.

Waldorf Salad

3 green apples
3 red apples
juice of one lemon
⅝ cup (150 ml) mayonnaise
salt and pepper
1 bunch celery
1 cup (120 g) chopped
    walnuts
lettuce leaves

1. Core and dice the apples but do not peel.
2. Combine the lemon juice, mayonnaise and salt and pepper. Mix well.
3. Add apples to the mayonnaise mixture and toss well.
4. Just before serving, add the celery which has been sliced and the walnuts to the apples and mix well.
5. Spoon salad onto a bed of lettuce leaves.

Serves 8.

Apple Tuna Salad

1 large can tuna fish
4 red apples
2 tablespoons lemon juice
4 stalks celery, chopped
1 tablespoon capers
½ cup (125 ml) mayonnaise
salt and pepper

1. Drain the tuna fish and break into bite-size pieces.
2. Core the apples (but do not peel) and dice them.
3. Sprinkle the lemon juice on the apples to keep them from discoloring.
4. Combine tuna fish with the apples, celery, capers and mayonnaise. Mix well.
5. Season to taste with the salt and pepper.

Serves 4-6.

Artichoke Hearts and Cheese Salad

2 cans artichoke hearts
  or 8 fresh artichoke hearts
  and bottoms
1 lb (500 g) cottage cheese
½ lb (250 g) cream cheese
3 grapefruit
mint sprigs
French Dressing (see index)

1. Drain artichoke hearts and set aside.
2. Mix the cottage cheese with the cream cheese and season with salt and pepper.
3. Fold in artichoke hearts and pile in the center of a platter.
4. Peel grapefruit and divide into segments.
5. Place grapefruit around and on top of cottage cheese mixture.
6. Pour French Dressing or a dressing of your choice over it all.
7. Garnish with mint sprigs.

Serves 6-8.

Anchovy Salad with Egg Dressing

1 lettuce
2 cans anchovy fillets
6 hard-boiled eggs
1 teaspoon salt
½ teaspoon pepper
1 teaspoon sugar
½ teaspoon paprika
1 teaspoon dry mustard

2 tablespoons cream
4 tablespoons olive
   or vegetable oil
1 tablespoon Worcestershire
   sauce
2 tablespoons vinegar
2 tablespoons chopped chives

1. Rice the egg yolks and mix with salt, pepper, sugar, paprika and dry mustard.
2. Gradually add cream, oil, Worcestershire Sauce and vinegar. Mix well.
3. Wash, drain and dry the lettuce and tear into bite-size pieces.
4. Put the lettuce in the salad bowl with the drained and cut up anchovy fillets.
5. Pour on dressing and toss thoroughly.
6. Sprinkle chopped egg whites on top.

Serves 6.

Celery Salad

1 bunch celery
1 onion, chopped finely
2 hard-boiled eggs,
   chopped very finely
3 teaspoons prepared mustard
salt and pepper
¼ cup (62.5 ml) olive
   or vegetable oil

1 tablespoon tarragon vinegar
1 tablespoon cream
2 tomatoes, sliced
½ cucumber, sliced
   (do not peel)

1. Wash the celery. Slice thinly.
2. Mix with the onion. Set aside.
3. Mix the finely chopped eggs with the mustard, oil, vinegar and cream. Season to taste with salt and pepper.
4. Pour dressing over the celery and onion mixture and toss lightly.
5. Garnish with slices of tomatoes and cucumber.

Serves 6-8.

Ham and Celery Salad

½ bunch celery, sliced
(Retain leaves for garnishing)
½ lb (250 g) lean ham, diced
½ cucumber, sliced
½ lb (250 g) cooked potatoes,
peeled and diced

1 cup (250 ml) mayonnaise
2 tablespoons capers
1 red pepper, finely chopped
2 hard-boiled eggs, sliced
lettuce

1. Lightly mix together the celery, ham, cucumber and potatoes.
2. Mix mayonnaise with capers and pepper.
3. Pour dressing over the celery and ham mixture and mix thoroughly.
4. Spoon salad onto lettuce leaves and garnish with sliced eggs and celery leaves.

Serves 4-6.

Celery Salad with Anchovies

1 bunch celery, cut into
one-inch (2.5 cm) pieces
¼ cup (62.5 ml) olive
or vegetable oil
3 tablespoons vinegar
salt and pepper
2 tomatoes, sliced
lettuce, one leaf for
each serving
3 hard-boiled eggs,
quartered

1 can anchovy fillets
¼ cup (62.5 ml) wine
vinegar
2 tablespoons tomato relish
1 teaspoon salt
¼ teaspoon pepper
½ cup (125 ml) olive
or vegetable oil

1. Marinate the celery in a mixture of the oil, vinegar, salt and pepper for at least two hours.
2. Place lettuce on serving dish. Arrange tomatoes on lettuce. Top with eggs and anchovy fillets.
3. Mix together vinegar, tomato relish, salt, pepper and oil.
4. Pour over each salad and serve immediately.

Serves 6-8.

Spinach Salad

1 bunch spinach
1 medium onion, chopped
½ cup diced celery
4 hard-boiled eggs, sliced

¼ teaspoon pepper
1 tablespoon capers
Garlic Dressing
 (see index)

1. Wash spinach very well, rinsing several times. Dry and tear into small pieces.
2. In a large bowl combine the spinach, onion, celery, eggs, salt and pepper.
3. Chill well.
4. Just before serving pour Garlic Dressing over the spinach salad and toss lightly.
5. Garnish with capers.

Serves 6.

Lamb Salad

1 lb (500 g) diced cooked lamb
1 cucumber, thinly sliced
2 tomatoes, diced
1 red apple, diced with skin

½ cup (60 g) chopped walnuts
salt and pepper
½ cup (125 g) sour cream

1. Combine the lamb, cucumber, tomatoes, apple and walnuts. Mix well.
2. Season to taste with salt and pepper.
3. Add sour cream and toss thoroughly.

Serves 4-6.

Stuffed Avocados

4 large avocados
6 hard-boiled eggs, riced
1 small jar caviar
1 can anchovies, chopped

1 tablespoon chopped chives
mayonnaise
chopped parsley

1. Cut avocados in halves.
2. Mix the eggs with the caviar, anchovies and chives.
3. Add enough mayonnaise to bind the mixture.
4. Fill avocados with the egg mixture and garnish with chopped parsley.

Chef's Salad

1 lettuce, washed, drained and dried	4 tomatoes, cut into wedges
1 green pepper, sliced	4 hard-boiled eggs
5 stalks celery, cut in one-inch (2.5 cm) pieces	strips of cold meat (turkey, chicken, ham, tongue, beef)
1 cucumber, sliced	strips of Swiss cheese
1 bunch radishes, sliced	French Dressing (see index)

1. In a large salad bowl place the lettuce, green pepper, celery, cucumber, radishes and tomatoes.
2. Arrange eggs, meat and cheese on top of vegetables.
3. Pour French Dressing or dressing of your choice over the salad.

Serves 6-8.

Chinese Cabbage Salad

1 chinese cabbage
1 bunch watercress
6 hard-boiled eggs
1 lb (500 g) cooked beets
3 tablespoons chopped chives
3 tablespoons chopped scallions

1. Cut cabbage crosswise in half-inch (10-mm) slices.
2. Place in a salad bowl lined with watercress.
3. Arrange over the top alternate slices of hard-boiled egg and slices of beets.
4. Sprinkle chives and scallions on salad.
5. Pour dressing of your choice on top.
6. Just before serving, toss lightly.

Serves 8.

Asparagus and Corn Salad

3 corn cobs
2 bunches asparagus
2 tablespoons capers
1 cup (250 ml) mayonnaise
juice of one lemon
1 teaspoon prepared horseradish
 sauce

salt and pepper
lettuce
2 hard-boiled eggs,
 sliced

1. Cook the corn in boiling water until tender. Drain and allow to cool.
2. Cook the asparagus in boiling water until just tender. Do not overcook.
3. Cut the asparagus into one-inch (2.5-cm) pieces.
4. Cut corn kernels from the cob and mix with asparagus and capers.
5. Mix the mayonnaise, lemon juice and horseradish sauce. Season to taste with salt and pepper. (Remember that the capers are salty so under- rather than over-salt the dressing.)
6. Pour dressing over the corn and asparagus mixture and toss lightly.
7. Place on individual lettuce leaves and garnish with slices of egg.

Serves 6-8.

Savory Mold

2 tablespoons gelatin
2½ cups (250 ml) beef stock
2 teaspoons dried parsley
 flakes
¼ lb (125 g) cooked peas

¼ lb (125 g) diced corned beef
¼ lb (125 g) diced salami
1 cucumber, sliced
2 hard-boiled eggs, sliced
1 tomato, chopped

1. Soak the gelatin in a little cold water. Add to the beef stock and parsley and mix well. Heat to dissolve gelatin.
2. Pour half the gelatin mixture in a ring mold and put in refrigerator to set.
3. When set, arrange peas, corned beef, salami, cucumber, eggs and tomato around the ring mold.
4. Pour on the remaining gelatin mixture, return to the refrigerator and allow to set.
5. When firm, unmold onto a bed of lettuce.

Serves 4-6.

East Coast Green Salad

1 green pepper, chopped
2 medium lettuces
salt and pepper
2 cups fried bread croutons
1½ cups (375 ml) olive oil
1 clove garlic, crushed
¼ cup (62.5 ml) Worcestershire Sauce

½ cup (125 ml) vinegar
juice of one lemon
2 tablespoons anchovies, cut and drained
½ cup (57 g) Parmesan cheese
2 eggs

1. Place pepper on washed, drained and dried lettuce in a salad bowl and toss. Sprinkle with salt and pepper.
2. Add croutons and mix well.
3. Mix olive oil with the garlic.
4. Pour oil, Worcestershire Sauce, vinegar and lemon juice on the salad and mix thoroughly.
5. Add anchovies and cheese and toss.
6. Boil eggs for 1½ minutes. Drop into salad and blend thoroughly. Serve immediately.

Serves 8-10.

Portuguese Salad

1 garlic, cut in half
1½ cup Julienne cut carrots
1 can artichoke hearts, quartered
1 red pepper, cut in strips

1 lettuce
½ lb (250 g) salami, cut into strips
French Dressing (see index)

1. Rub the inside of the salad bowl with the garlic.
2. Mix the carrots, artichoke hearts and pepper together in the bowl.
3. Wash, drain and dry the lettuce. Tear into bite-size pieces. Add to the other vegetables and toss well.
4. Pour a highly seasoned French Dressing over the salad and mix thoroughly.
5. Place salami on top of salad.

Serves 6.

Lettuce and Chicory Salad

2 lettuces
1 bunch chicory
1 cucumber, sliced
1 green pepper, sliced

1 cup chopped celery
1 can anchovies, drained
French Dressing (see index)

1. Wash and drain lettuce and chicory.
2. Tear lettuce and cut chicory in small pieces.
3. Combine with cucumber, celery and green pepper.
4. Place in bowl, pour over French Dressing and toss lightly.
5. Garnish with anchovies.

Serves 8-10.

Epicurean Green Salad

2 lettuces
1 green pepper, chopped
1 cup chopped celery
1 clove garlic
2 eggs, boiled for 1½ minutes
1 cup (250 ml) olive
or vegetable oil
½ cup (125 ml) vinegar

2 tablespoons mayonnaise
2 teaspoons prepared mustard
2 teaspoons Worcestershire
sauce
½ teaspoon salt
¼ teaspoon pepper
½ cup (57 g) Parmesan cheese,
grated

1. Wash and drain lettuce.
2. Rub salad bowl with the garlic clove.
3. Put lettuce, pepper and celery in the bowl and mix well.
4. Break eggs over the mixed salad and toss lightly.
5. Combine remaining ingredients except the Parmesan cheese and beat well.
6. Pour over the salad and toss lightly.
7. Sprinkle Parmesan cheese over the salad.

Serves 8-10.

Japanese Egg Salad

½ cup (105 g) rice
½ onion, chopped finely
1 cup (250 ml) French Dressing
(see index)
1 lb (500 g) cooked shrimp
6 hard-boiled eggs

lettuce leaves
4 sweet gherkins
2 tablespoons tomato sauce
1 tablespoon capers, chopped
1 tablespoon chopped chives

1. Cook and drain the rice.
2. Add onion, ½ cup of dressing, shrimp and three eggs, diced. Mix carefully. Chill.
3. Put lettuce leaves on a platter and place egg mixture on top.
4. Sprinkle gherkins around the edge of the salad.
5. Grate the remaining egg white and yolks separately. Sprinkle over salad.
6. Mix the remaining ½ cup of dressing with tomato sauce, capers and chives and pour over the salad.

Serves 4-6.

Hot Egg Salad

2 tablespoons (40 g) butter
or margarine
2 tablespoons flour
1½ teaspoons salt
½ teaspoon pepper
1 cup (250 ml) milk
2 lbs (1 kg) diced cooked
potatoes

2 medium onions, minced
1 red pepper, chopped
1 cup chopped celery
½ cup (75 g) stuffed olives
6 hard-boiled eggs, quartered
½ cup French Dressing
(see index)

1. Melt butter in a large saucepan. Blend in flour and seasonings.
2. Slowly add the milk, stirring constantly. Continue cooking and stirring until thickened.
3. Add potatoes and heat gently.
4. Before serving, add the remaining ingredients. Toss gently.

Serves 4-6.

Crab Salad

4 oz (125 g)
    black olives
4 stalks celery, chopped
1 large can crabmeat

½ cup (125 ml) mayonnaise
2 tablespoons tomato paste
1 tablespoon lemon juice
salt
cayenne

1. Cut the olives in halves and remove the pits.
2. Mix the olives, celery and crabmeat together.
3. Blend the mayonnaise, tomato paste and lemon juice. Season to taste with salt and cayenne.
4. Toss the crabmeat mixture in the dressing.
5. Chill well before serving.

Serves 4.

Mushroom Salad

1 lb (500 g) mushrooms
juice of two lemons
¼ cup (625 ml) olive oil

2 tablespoons chopped parsley
salt and pepper
1 cup chopped celery

1. Wipe the mushrooms with a damp cloth. Quarter the mushrooms.
2. Mix the lemon juice with the olive oil and chopped parsley.
3. Season to taste with salt and pepper.
4. Pour over the mushrooms and toss lightly.
5. Chill for at least one hour.
6. Just before serving toss in the celery. Mix well.

Serves 6-8.

Garden Cole Slaw

¼ cabbage, shredded
½ cup sliced radishes
½ cucumber, sliced
2 stalks celery, sliced
2 tablespoons chopped parsley
2 tablespoons grated onion

1 cup (250 ml) mayonnaise
2 tablespoons tarragon vinegar
2 tablespoons prepared mustard
½ cup (125 ml) cream
1 teaspoon salt
½ teaspoon pepper

1. Toss together cabbage, radishes, cucumber, celery, parsley and onion.
2. Combine mayonnaise with the vinegar, mustard, cream, salt and pepper. Beat well.
3. Pour over cole slaw and mix well.

Serves 6-8.

Orange and Watercress Salad

1 medium lettuce
2 bunches watercress
6 oranges
2 tablespoons chopped mint
1 tablespoon grated orange peel
Lemon Dressing (see index)

1. Wash and drain lettuce and watercress.
2. Peel and slice oranges into rounds.
3. Combine watercress, oranges, mint and orange peel. Mix well.
4. Place lettuce in bowl and cover with the watercress and orange mixture.
5. Pour Lemon Dressing over and serve immediately.

Serves 6-8.

Vegetables Salad

1 cauliflower	1 lettuce
2 bunches asparagus	Sour Cream Dressing
1 lb (500 g) cherry tomatoes	(see index)

1. Cut cauliflower into flowerets. Cook in boiling salted water for 3-5 minutes. Drain and chill.
2. Wash asparagus well. Cook until tender but still firm. Drain and cut into one-inch (2.5-cm) pieces. Chill.
3. Serve the cauliflower, asparagus and cherry tomatoes on top of the lettuce.
4. Pour Sour Cream Dressing over it all.

Serves 8.

Hot String Bean Salad

1 lb (500 g) green beans	1 cup (250 ml) bean liquid
½ onion, minced	½ tablespoon sugar
2 tablespoons olive oil	salt and paprika
2 tablespoons vinegar	chopped chives

1. Cook the beans in boiling water for 5-7 minutes. Drain and reserve one cup of the liquid.
2. Mix the onion, the olive oil, vinegar and sugar with the bean liquid. Season to taste with salt and paprika.
3. Pour over beans while still hot. (May also be served cold.)

Serves 4-6.

Apple-Cabbage Salad

1 Savoy cabbage
5 red apples
½ lb (250 g) cheddar cheese
salt and pepper

¾ cup (187 ml) mayonnaise
¼ cup (62.5 ml) vinegar
1 tablespoon prepared mustard
pinch sugar

1. Wash and drain cabbage. Shred finely. Retain outer leaves.
2. Wash apples. Core but do not peel. Dice the apples.
3. Grate cheese.
4. Combine cabbage, apples and cheese. Mix well. Add salt and pepper to taste.
5. Beat mayonnaise, vinegar, mustard and sugar together.
6. Pour dressing over salad and toss lightly.
7. Line the salad bowl with the outer leaves of the cabbage and fill with the salad.

Serves 8.

Cottage Cheese-Peach Salad

1 cup (250 g) cottage cheese
2 tablespoons raisins
4 peaches or 8 canned
   peach halves
3 tablespoons (30 g)
   chopped walnuts
lettuce

1. Mix the cottage cheese with the raisins. Set aside.
2. Peel and halve the peaches. Place on a bed of lettuce.
3. Spoon cottage cheese and raisins mixture onto peaches.
4. Garnish with chopped walnuts.

Serves 4.

Bacon and Egg Salad

12 strips bacon
4 hard-boiled eggs
½ cup (125 ml) white vinegar
2 tablespoons Worcestershire sauce
½ cup (125 ml) olive
  or vegetable oil
½ cup (125 ml) lemon juice

1½ teaspoons salt
½ teaspoon black pepper
½ teaspoon paprika
1 lettuce
1 green pepper
1 bunch watercress
2 stalks celery, chopped

1. Cook the bacon until brown and crispy. Drain and crumble.
2. Quarter the eggs.
3. Blend vinegar, Worcestershire sauce, oil, lemon juice, salt, pepper and paprika. Set aside.
4. Wash and drain lettuce. Chop green pepper. Cut off hard stems of watercress.
5. Mix lettuce which has been broken into bite-size pieces, the pepper, watercress, celery, bacon and eggs.
6. Pour dressing over all and toss lightly.

Serves 8.

Cabbage Salad

1 tomato, chopped
4 scallions, chopped (white
  and green parts)
½ teaspoon salt

½ cup (125 ml) mayonnaise
2 tablespoons lemon juice
1 cup chopped celery
¼ cabbage, shredded

1. Combine tomato, scallions, salt, mayonnaise and lemon juice. Mix well and chill.
2. Combine celery and cabbage.
3. Pour dressing over the salad and toss lightly.

Serves 4-6.

Bacon and Lettuce Salad

1 large lettuce
½ lb (250 g) bacon,
  cut into small bits
¼ cup (62.5 ml) olive oil
1 tablespoon brown sugar
3 tablespoons vinegar

1. Wash, drain and dry the lettuce. Tear into bite-size pieces and put in a salad bowl.
2. Fry the bacon until crispy.
3. Add the sugar and vinegar and while still hot pour over the lettuce.
4. Serve immediately.

Serves 6-8.

Scrambled Egg Salad

6 eggs
salt and pepper
1 teaspoon chopped mint
1 teaspoon chopped parsley
2 tablespoons (40 g) butter
  or margarine

3 medium carrots
1 medium onion
4 tomatoes
½ cup chopped celery
½ cucumber
French Dressing (see index)

1. Lightly beat the eggs, season with salt and pepper and add the chopped herbs. Scramble in the butter. When cooked turn off heat and allow the eggs to cool. When cold, cut into small pieces.
2. Grate the carrots, chop the onion, slice the tomatoes and cucumber and mix together all these ingredients with the chopped celery.
3. Gently mix the egg pieces with the vegetables.
4. Pour on French Dressing and toss very gently.

Serves 6-8.

Dairy Cheese Salad

6 large tomatoes
¼ lb (125 g) cream cheese
anchovy paste
lettuce

cottage cheese
3 hard-boiled eggs, chopped
1¼ cups (300 g) sour cream
caviar

1. Peel tomatoes and cut off a slice from the top.
2. Blend cream cheese with anchovy paste and spread this mixture on top of each tomato.
3. Place a bed of lettuce on individual dishes. Place a scoop of cottage cheese on top of lettuce.
4. Put tomato on top of cottage cheese.
5. Sprinkle the chopped egg over each tomato.
6. Mix the sour cream with the caviar and pour over the tomatoes.

Serves 6.

Italian Salad

1 cucumber, sliced
5 tomatoes, cut into
  small chunks
6 scallions, sliced (white
  and green parts)
1 bunch watercress, washed,
  drained and dried
1 lettuce, washed,
  drained and dried

¼ lb (125 g) blue cheese
1 small can anchovies
1 small jar caviar
3 tablespoons olive oil
1 tablespoon lemon juice
  or vinegar
1 clove garlic, crushed
salt and pepper

1. Mix the cucumber, tomatoes, scallions, watercress and lettuce.
2. Cream the cheese, cut the anchovies into small pieces and add both these ingredients to the caviar, oil, lemon juice and garlic.
3. Season to taste with salt and pepper and pour over the vegetables. Toss thoroughly.

Serves 6-8.

Raisin and Carrot Salad

1 cup (165 g) raisins
2 oranges
1½ lb (750 g) carrots
1 onion, minced

½ cup (125 ml) mayonnaise
2 tablespoons lemon juice
1 teaspoon brown sugar
½ teaspoon salt

1. Place raisins in a bowl and cover with boiling water. Allow to stand until plump — about five minutes. Drain well.
2. Peel the orange and divide in segments. Cut segments into chunks.
3. Grate the carrots and add them with the onion to the raisins and oranges. Mix well.
4. Blend the mayonnaise with the lemon juice, sugar and salt.
5. Pour the dressing over the salad and toss well.

Serves 4.

Leek and Tomato Salad

6 leeks
6 medium tomatoes
1 lettuce
1 clove garlic, crushed
1 teaspoon chopped dill
1 teaspoon chopped basil

1 teaspoon chopped chervil
3 tablespoons olive
or vegetable oil
1 tablespoon lemon juice
1 tablespoon chopped capers

1. Wash the leeks and slice the white part coarsely.
2. Quarter the tomatoes.
3. Wash, drain and dry the lettuce.
4. Rub the garlic around the salad bowl.
5. Break up lettuce and arrange in bowl.
6. Place the leeks and tomatoes on the lettuce.
7. Sprinkle with dill, basil and chervil.
8. Mix the oil, lemon juice and capers and pour over the salad.

Serves 6.

Ambrosia Salad

3 bananas, sliced
3 oranges, diced
½ lb (250 g) seedless grapes
½ cup (75 g) chopped dates
juice of one lemon

½ cup (45 g) desiccated
  coconut
1 cup (250 ml) cream
mint

1. Combine bananas, orange pieces, grapes and dates in a bowl.
2. Pour lemon juice over the fruit and toss lightly. Chill.
3. Add coconut. Mix well.
4. Whip cream and fold through the fruit. Chill until ready to serve.
5. Garnish with mint leaves.

Serves 6.

Herb Slaw

¼ cabbage, finely shredded
3 medium onions, sliced
3 carrots, grated
2 cups chopped celery
½ cup (125 ml) vinegar
½ cup (125 ml) olive
  or vegetable oil
¼ cup sugar

1 cup (250 ml) water
2 teaspoons salt
¼ teaspoon each, basil,
  dill seed and tarragon
½ teaspoon celery seed
  and dried parsley
cucumber
tomatoes

1. Mix cabbage, onion, carrots and celery. Chill.
2. Mix vinegar, oil, sugar, water and seasonings together.
3. Just before serving, pour over the mixed vegetables and toss well.
4. Garnish with cucumber slices and tomato wedges.

Serves 8.

Apple and Chicken Salad

1 lb (500 g) cooked chicken meat	⅓ cup (125 ml) mayonnaise
3 red apples	⅓ cup (83 ml) cream, whipped
¼ cup (62.5 ml) lemon juice	1 teaspoon salt
5 stalks celery, chopped	¼ teaspoon pepper
1 cup (115 g) slivered almonds	2 teaspoons capers, chopped
	1 lettuce

1. Core the apples but do not peel. Cut the apples into chunks and dip in the lemon juice to prevent discoloring.
2. Combine the chicken, apples, celery and almonds. Mix well.
3. Mix together the mayonnaise with the remaining lemon juice, whipped cream, salt, pepper and chopped capers.
4. Add to the chicken and apple mixture and blend thoroughly.
5. Spoon salad onto a bed of lettuce.

Serves 6.

Beets and Apple Mold

1 packet of cherry gelatin	1 lb (500 g) cooked beets
1¼ cups (300 ml) boiling water	2 green apples
½ cup (125 ml) vinegar	½ cup chopped celery
2 tablespoons lemon juice	½ cup (60 g) chopped walnuts

1. Dissolve the gelatin in the 1¼ cups boiling water.
2. Combine the vinegar and lemon juice and enough water to make up to 1½ cups.
3. Dice the beets. Core (do not peel) the apples and cut into slices.
4. Put the walnuts in the base of a ring mold, then the beets and apple.
5. Carefully pour on the gelatin and refrigerate until firm.
6. Unmold onto a bed of lettuce.

Serves 6.

Potato Apple Salad

6 medium potatoes	¼ cup (62.5 ml) olive oil
4 medium red apples	¼ cup (62.5 ml) white wine
1 large onion, chopped	1 teaspoon lemon juice
1 cup chopped celery	salt and pepper
1 tablespoon capers	
2 tablespoons chopped green pepper	

1. Cook the potatoes in boiling water until just tender. Drain and cool. Cut into bite-size pieces.
2. Core the apples (do not peel) and cut into chunks.
3. Mix the potatoes, apples, onion, celery, capers, and green pepper.
4. Mix the oil with the white wine and lemon juice. Season to taste with salt and pepper.
5. Pour over the potato and apple mixture and toss gently.

Serves 6-8.

Beet Salad

1 lb (500 g) beets, cooked	½ cup (125 g) yoghurt
2 onions, sliced	1 teaspoon salt
1 cucumber, sliced	½ teaspoon caraway seeds
1 teaspoon sugar	2 tablespoons lemon juice

1. Peel and slice the beets.
2. Mix the beets with the onions, cucumber and sugar.
3. Mix the yoghurt with the salt, caraway seeds and lemon juice.
4. Gently mix the yoghurt with the beets mixture.

Serves 4-6.

Tongue Salad

4 medium potatoes,
  cooked and diced
1 cup chopped celery
1 green pepper, chopped
1 cup green beans
1 lb (500 g) cooked tongue,
  diced

¼ cup (62.5 ml) French Dressing
  (see index)
½ lettuce
½ cup (125 ml) mayonnaise

1. Combine the potatoes, celery, green pepper and slightly cooked green beans. Mix well. Add the tongue.
2. Sprinkle on the French Dressing. Toss well and allow to marinate for one hour.
3. Add the tongue mixture to the lettuce.
4. Add the mayonnaise and mix well.

Serves 6.

Salami Salad

½ lb (250 g) salami, cubed
4 potatoes, cooked and cubed
1 red pepper, chopped
1 cucumber, chopped
2 tablespoons chives, chopped

2 tablespoons chopped parsley
1 onion, thinly sliced
1 cup chopped celery
lettuce leaves
Italian Dressing (see index)

1. Combine all the ingredients except the lettuce and the dressing. Mix well.
2. Add dressing and toss well. Allow to marinate in the dressing for one hour.
3. Serve on a bed of crisp lettuce leaves.

Serves 6.

Grapefruit and Avocado Salad

2 lettuces
2 grapefruit
2 avocados
2 persimmons
¼ cup chopped mint

1. Wash and drain the lettuce.
2. Cut the grapefruit into segments.
3. Peel the avocados and cut into cubes.
4. Cut the persimmons into slices.
5. Combine all the ingredients and toss lightly with French Dressing (see index).
6. Garnish with mint.

Spring Salad Mold

2 tablespoons unflavored gelatin
½ cup (125 ml) cold water
1 green pepper, chopped
4 stalks celery, chopped
3 carrots, chopped
3 medium onions, thinly sliced

1 lb (500 g) tomatoes
½ cup (125 ml) vinegar
¼ cup sugar
½ teaspoon salt
cucumber slices, celery leaves for garnishing

1. Soak the gelatin in the cold water.
2. Combine green pepper, celery, carrots, and onions and set aside.
3. Put tomatoes in a saucepan and cover with boiling water. Remove from saucepan, peel and quarter. Return to saucepan.
4. Bring tomatoes to a boil. Add gelatin and dissolve. Cool and add remaining ingredients.
5. Add mixed vegetables and blend thoroughly.
6. Pour into a wet ring mold and chill until firm.
7. Unmold and garnish with cucumber slices and celery leaves.

Serves 8.

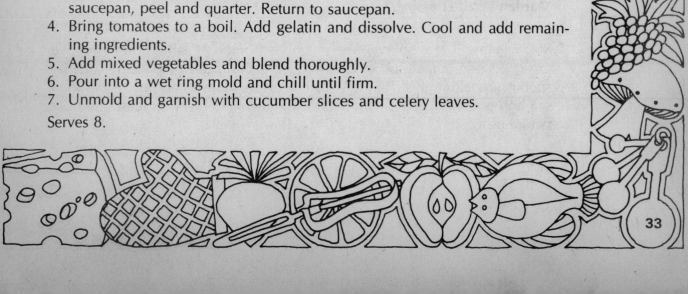

Rice Confetti Salad

6 cups cooked rice	6 hard-boiled eggs, chopped
1 onion, minced	2 teaspoons salt
1 cup chopped celery	½ teaspoon pepper
2 slices of bacon, cooked and crumbled	1½ cups (375 ml) mayonnaise
	2 teaspoons prepared mustard
1 cup sweet pickle relish	lettuce leaves
½ cup diced red pepper	cherry tomatoes

1. Blend all ingredients together thoroughly.
2. Serve on lettuce leaves and garnish with cherry tomatoes.

Serves 10.

(Note: one cup uncooked rice makes three cups cooked rice.)

Grapefruit-Tuna Salad

1 large can tuna fish
1 cucumber, sliced
3 cups grapefruit sections
3 tomatoes, sliced
Garden Salad Dressing

1. Mound chunks of tuna in middle of platter.
2. Arrange cucumber slices around edge of platter.
3. Fill in area around the tuna fish with grapefruit section and tomatoes.
4. Pour dressing over all.

Serves 4.

Garden Salad Dressing:

Mix together 3 tablespoons finely chopped onion, 1 tablespoon chopped green pepper, 1 tablespoon chopped fresh basil, dill or parsley, 6 tablespoons grapefruit juice, ¼ cup water, 2 tablespoons salad oil, ¼ teaspoon salt and pinch of pepper. Allow dressing flavors to blend at least one hour before using.

Tuna Macaroni Salad

3 cups cooked macaroni
1 large can tuna fish, drained
1 can artichoke hearts, drained
3 tomatoes, diced
1 teaspoon salt
¼ teaspoon pepper

1 clove garlic, crushed
¼ teaspoon paprika
½ cup (125 ml) salad oil
¼ cup (62.5 ml) vinegar
spinach leaves

1. Combine tuna, macaroni, halved artichoke hearts and tomatoes. Toss lightly.
2. Mix together salt, pepper, garlic, paprika, oil and vinegar.
3. Pour dressing over tuna and macaroni mixture and toss thoroughly. Chill until ready to serve.
4. Serve on well washed spinach leaves.

Serves 4-6.

Beany Egg Salad

6 hard-boiled eggs,
  coarsely chopped
1 large can three-bean mix
3 scallions, chopped
  (white and green parts)
2 tablespoons chili sauce

2 tablespoons mayonnaise
1 teaspoon prepared mustard
1 teaspoon salt
3 slices bacon, cooked and crumbled
4 tablespoons chopped parsley

1. Drain beans. Rinse under cold water and drain thoroughly.
2. Add remaining ingredients and toss lightly.
3. Serve chilled.

Serves 6.

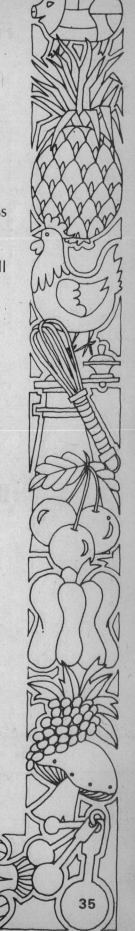

Frozen Crab Salad

½ lb (250 g) cream cheese
1 cup (250 ml) mayonnaise
1 teaspoon Tabasco sauce
½ teaspoon salt
1 cup (250 ml) cream, whipped
2 cups crab meat

1 cup chopped celery
1 cup chopped green pepper
½ cup grated carrot
1 tablespoon chopped onion
lettuce leaves

1. Soften cream cheese. Blend with mayonnaise, Tabasco sauce and salt.
2. Fold in whipped cream. Blend in crab, celery, green pepper, carrot and onion.
3. Pour into two freezer trays. Freeze until solid — about 6 to 8 hours.
4. Remove from freezer and allow to stand at room temperature for about 15 minutes before slicing. Serve on lettuce leaves.

Serves 8.

Bombay Salad

1 cup diced chestnuts
1 small can button mushrooms
1½ cups diced, cooked
   duckling
¼ cup (62.5 ml) French
   Dressing (see index)

1 cup diced celery
¼ (62.5 ml) cup mayonnaise
1 teaspoon salt
curry powder to taste
lettuce leaves
shredded coconut

1. Combine chestnuts, mushrooms and duckling in a bowl. Pour on French Dressing and mix well. Cover and allow to marinate in the refrigerator for several hours.
2. When ready to serve, drain off excess dressing. Add celery.
3. Blend together the mayonnaise, salt and curry powder. Add to the duckling and mix well.
4. Serve over crisp lettuce and garnish with shredded coconut.

Serves 4.

Jellied Party Loaf

1½ lb (750 g) luncheon meat
1½ cups (375 ml) chicken stock
1 tablespoon gelatin
1 tablespoon grated onion
½ teaspoon gravy maker
1½ lb (750 g) cooked chicken
   or veal
1 tablespoon gelatin
½ cup (125 ml) chicken stock
1 cup (250 ml) sour cream
1 teaspoon salt
¼ teaspoon pepper
6 teaspoons marjoram
2 tablespoons chopped stuffed
   olives
2 teaspoons prepared horseradish
   sauce
lettuce leaves, watercress
   and stuffed olives to garnish

1. Put luncheon meat through meat grinder using fine cutter.
2. Soak the gelatin in ½ cup of the chicken stock. Let stand for five minutes, then dissolve over very low heat. Add remaining stock, onion and gravy maker. Pour over the ground meat and mix well. Chill until beginning to thicken.
3. Put chicken or veal through meat grinder.
4. Soften gelatin in ½ cup chicken stock for five minutes. Dissolve over very low heat. Add to sour cream. Add salt, pepper, marjoram, chopped stuffed olives and horseradish sauce. Pour over ground chicken or veal and mix thoroughly.
5. Pour into an oiled loaf pan. Spread evenly.
6. Carefully pour the luncheon meat mixture over the chicken or veal mixture. Chill until firm.
7. Unmold onto lettuce leaves. Garnish with watercress and stuffed olives.

Serves 12.

Ham and Cheese Salad

1 lb (500 g) Gruyere cheese	salt and pepper
1 lb (500 g) ham, diced	1 lettuce
8 tablespoons olive or salad oil	2 tablespoons chopped parsley
3 tablespoons vinegar	1 tablespoon chopped chives

1. Combine the cheese and ham in a large bowl.
2. Mix the oil with the vinegar. Season to taste with salt and pepper.
3. Pour dressing over the cheese and ham and marinate for at least one hour in the refrigerator.
4. Wash, drain and dry the lettuce. Break up into bite-size pieces. Place in a salad bowl.
5. Put cheese and ham in bowl with the lettuce and toss lightly.
6. Sprinkle with parsley and chives.

Serves 8.

Tomato-Potato Salad

6 tomatoes, peeled, seeded and chopped	juice of one lemon
6 new potatoes, cooked and diced (with skin)	1 lettuce
1 avocado, peeled, seeded and diced	French Dressing (see index)
	1 onion, chopped

1. Combine tomatoes and potatoes.
2. Dip the avocado in the lemon juice. Drain.
3. Add the avocado to the tomatoes and potatoes.
4. Wash, drain and dry the lettuce. Place in a salad bowl.
5. Put tomato mixture on top of the lettuce. Pour French Dressing on top and garnish with chopped onion.

Serves 8.

Apple Cabbage Bowl

1 medium cabbage	¼ teaspoon pepper
2 cups puréed apples	½ teaspoon dry mustard
1 cup chopped celery	1 teaspoon caraway seeds
1 small onion, chopped	1 cup mayonnaise (250 ml)
½ green pepper, chopped	½ cup (125 g) sour cream
½ red pepper, chopped	2 tablespoons vinegar
1 teaspoon salt	slivered almonds

1. Rinse cabbage well. Do not remove outer leaves.
2. Slice top off cabbage and hollow out head, leaving a thin, bowl-like shell.
3. Shred or chop cabbage to make 5 to 6 cups.
4. Mix cabbage with puréed apples, celery, onion, peppers, salt and pepper, dry mustard and caraway seeds.
5. Mix together the mayonnaise, sour cream, and vinegar.
6. Pour this dressing onto the cabbage mixture and toss thoroughly. Chill until ready to serve.
7. When ready to serve, put slaw into cabbage shell and garnish with slivered almonds.

Serves 6-8.

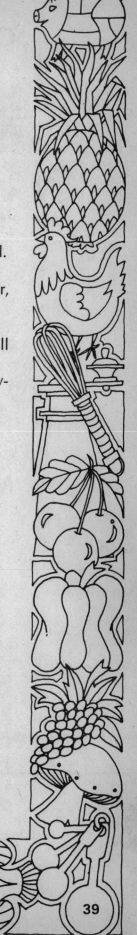

Carrot Salad with Nuts and Raisins

1 lb (500 g) carrots	¼ teaspoon pepper
½ cup raisins	2 teaspoons grated lemon rind
½ cup chopped peanuts	2 tablespoons lemon juice
1 teaspoon salt	1¼ cups (300 g) sour cream

1. Coarsely grate carrots.
2. Mix carrots with the raisins, peanuts, salt and pepper.
3. Blend the lemon rind, lemon juice and sour cream.
4. Pour over the carrot mixture and toss thoroughly.

Serves 4.

Macaroni Salad

1½ cups macaroni	4 tablespoons chopped parsley
2 tablespoons lemon juice	¼ lb (125 g) stuffed olives, sliced
1 tablespoon olive or salad oil	1 teaspoon salt
2 tablespoons chopped chives	4 tablespoons sour cream
2 teaspoons grated onion	½ red pepper, chopped
1 cup diced celery	lettuce leaves

1. Cook the macaroni in boiling salted water until tender. Drain.
2. Mix together the lemon juice and oil. Pour onto the macaroni and mix well.
3. Mix together the chives, onion, celery, parsley, olives, salt, sour cream and pepper.
4. Add to the macaroni and mix thoroughly.
5. Spoon macaroni salad onto lettuce leaves and chill.

Serves 6.

Chicken Liver Salad

1 lb (500 g) chicken livers, diced
3 tablespoons (60 g) butter or margarine
salt
1 clove garlic, halved
1 lettuce, washed, drained and dried

1 onion, thinly sliced
3 hard-boiled eggs
¼ lb (125 g) blue cheese, crumbled
½ cup well-seasoned French Dressing (see index)

1. Cook the chicken livers in the butter until lightly browned. Season to taste with salt. Cool.
2. Rub the salad bowl with the garlic clove.
3. Combine all the ingredients including the chicken livers.
4. Pour the dressing over the salad and toss lightly.

Serves 6.

Veal Salad

1 lb (500 g) diced cooked veal
½ cup French Dressing (see index)
2 teaspoons soy sauce
½ lb (250 g) bean sprouts
1 onion, chopped

1 teaspoon salt
¼ teaspoon pepper
½ cup (125 ml) mayonnaise
lettuce leaves

1. Marinate veal in a mixture of the dressing and soy sauce for one hour.
2. Add bean sprouts to veal and mix well. Allow to marinate for ½ hour.
3. Add onion, salt and pepper and mayonnaise. Toss thoroughly.
4. Place salad on a bed of lettuce leaves.

Serves 4-6.

41

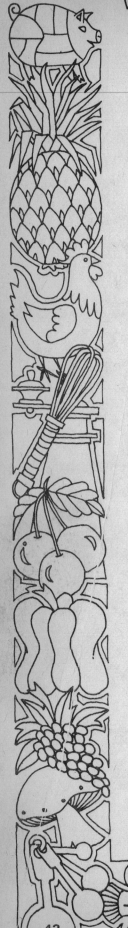

Lima Bean Salad

2 cups dried lima beans
2 small onions, sliced
2 cloves garlic, crushed
1 teaspoon salt
¼ teaspoon pepper
olive or salad oil

6 scallions, sliced
(white and green parts)
2 tablespoons vinegar
3 teaspoons lemon juice
lettuce leaves

1. Soak lima beans overnight in cold water. Drain. Cover with cold water and bring to a boil. Reduce heat and simmer for about 2 hours or until beans are tender. Drain.
2. Place onions and garlic in a bowl with the salt and pepper. Cover with oil and marinate for one hour.
3. Add lima beans and scallions and mix well.
4. Sprinkle vinegar and lemon juice over the lima bean mixture and toss thoroughly.
5. Wash, drain and dry lettuce leaves. Line a salad bowl with the lettuce leaves and spoon lima bean salad into bowl. Serve at room temperature or chilled.

Serves 6.

Oriental Rice Salad

½ teaspoon powdered saffron
¼ teaspoon powdered cumin
¼ cup (62.5 ml) dry white wine
2½ cups (600 ml) chicken stock
1½ cups (315 g) rice
½ green pepper, chopped coarsely
½ red pepper, chopped coarsely
1 small onion, chopped

salt and pepper

Dressing:
8 tablespoons olive or salad oil
3 tablespoons vinegar
2 tablespoons chopped parsley
salt and pepper

1. Dissolve the saffron and cumin in the wine and chicken stock. Pour into a large saucepan and add the rice, peppers, onion and salt and pepper to taste. Cover and simmer until all the liquid is absorbed (about 20 minutes).
2. Mix oil, vinegar and parsley. Season to taste with salt and pepper. Pour onto hot rice. Cool.

Serves 4-6.

Brussels Sprouts Salad

2 lb (1 kg) small Brussels sprouts
1 onion, chopped
2 tablespoons chopped parsley

½ cup chopped cooked beets
lettuce leaves
French Dressing (see index)

1. Cook Brussels sprouts in salted boiling water until tender. Do not over-cook. Drain and cool.
2. Combine the Brussels sprouts with the onion and parsley. Toss in French Dressing.
3. Wash, drain and dry the lettuce leaves. Line a salad bowl with the leaves.
4. Put Brussels sprouts mixture on top of lettuce.
5. Arrange the beets around the edges.
(Use more French Dressing if desired.)
Serves 6-8.

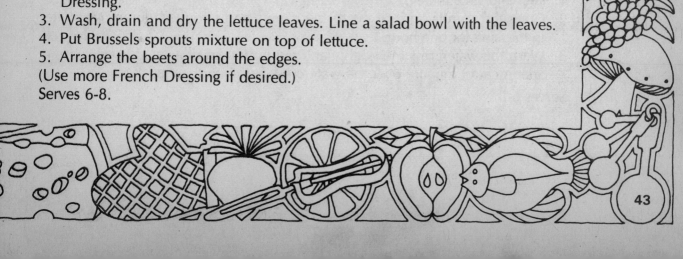

Cucumber and Mint Salad

2 large cucumbers
1 cup (250 g) plain yoghurt
1 tablespoon lemon juice
2 tablespoons chopped mint
lettuce leaves
sprigs of mint

1. Peel and slice the cucumbers.
2. Mix the yoghurt with the lemon juice. Add the mint and mix well.
3. Pour the yoghurt mixture onto the cucumbers and mix well.
4. Wash, drain and dry the lettuce leaves. Place in the bottom of a salad bowl.
5. Spoon cucumbers on top of lettuce.
6. Garnish with sprigs of mint.

Serves 6.

Egg and Carrot Salad

6 hard-boiled eggs
1 lb (500 g) young carrots
2 tablespoons capers
1 small onion, chopped
1 bunch watercress
French Dressing (see index)

1. Peel and slice the eggs.
2. Grate the carrots and mix with the capers and chopped onion. Marinate in dressing for one hour.
3. Wash the watercress thoroughly and put in bottom of a salad bowl.
4. Spoon carrot mixture over the watercress and then the egg slices.

Serves 6-8.

Orange and Onion Salad

6 oranges
2 medium onions
lettuce leaves

Dressing:
6 tablespoons olive or salad oil
3 tablespoons vinegar
1 clove garlic, crushed
1 teaspoon salt
½ teaspoon dry mustard
1 teaspoon sugar

1. Wash, drain and dry the lettuce leaves. Arrange them in the bottom of a salad bowl.
2. Peel the oranges and carefully remove all the pith. Slice thinly in rounds. Arrange on top of the lettuce.
3. Peel the onion and slice thinly. Arrange on top of oranges.
4. Mix together all the ingredients for the dressing. Beat well
5. Before serving pour dressing over the salad.

Serves 6.

Russian Tomato Salad

16 small tomatoes, peeled
1½ cups (375 ml) cream, whipped
1 cup (250 ml) mayonnaise
2 tablespoons prepared horseradish

4 tablespoons chopped parsley
salt and pepper
paprika

1. Combine whipped cream with mayonnaise, horseradish and parsley. Season to taste with salt and pepper.
2. When ready to serve, arrange tomatoes on a dish and spoon dressing on top. Sprinkle with paprika.

Serves 6-8.

Curried Chicken Salad

1 cup (210 g) rice	curry powder to taste
7½ cups (1.8 liters) salted water	½ teaspoon salt
1 lb (500 g) cooked chicken meat	¼ teaspoon pepper
1 small cauliflower	3 tablespoons cream
1 red pepper, chopped	1 green pepper, cut into strips
3 tablespoons salad oil	2 stalks celery, sliced
1 tablespoon vinegar	2 medium onions, sliced
small clove garlic, crushed	lettuce leaves
½ cup (125 ml) mayonnaise	

1. Cook the rice in boiling salted water until tender. Drain very well and allow to dry in a warm place.
2. Cut the chicken into bite-size pieces.
3. Cut the cauliflower into flowerets.
4. Combine the oil, vinegar and crushed garlic and pour this dressing over the rice, cauliflower and red pepper. Set aside.
5. Combine the mayonnaise, curry powder, salt, pepper and cream. Add the chicken and toss well.
6. Combine the rice mixture, the green pepper, celery, onions and the chicken.
7. Spoon the salad onto a bed of lettuce leaves.

Serves 6-8.

Avocado Salad

3 avocados	3 tablespoons olive oil
2 tablespoons lemon juice	1-2 tablespoons vinegar
1 cup chopped celery	2 teaspoons French mustard
1 onion, chopped finely	1 clove garlic, crushed
2 tablespoons chopped parsley	salt and pepper

1. Peel and cube the avocados. Toss in lemon juice to prevent discoloring. Remove from lemon juice.
2. Mix the avocados with the celery, onion and parsley.
3. Combine the oil, vinegar, mustard, garlic and salt and pepper. Mix thoroughly. Pour over the avocados and toss gently.

Serves 6.

Stuffed Zucchini Salad

8 large zucchini
1 medium onion, finely chopped
1 clove garlic, crushed
½ cup (125 ml) French Dressing (see index)
4 tomatoes, peeled, seeded and chopped
½ green pepper, chopped

½ medium onion, finely chopped
2 tablespoons capers, chopped
2 teaspoons chopped parsley
1 teaspoon chopped chives
salt and pepper

1. Simmer zucchini in salted water for about five minutes. Cut them in half lengthwise and scoop out seeds. Be careful not to break the skin.
2. Mix together onion and garlic and spread over zucchini. Sprinkle with ¼ cup of the French dressing. Cover and allow to marinate for several hours.
3. Mix together tomatoes, pepper, onion, capers, parsley and chives. Season to taste with salt and pepper.
4. When ready to serve, remove the onion and garlic mixture from the zucchini. Fill the zucchini with the tomato mixture. Sprinkle with the remaining French dressing.

Serves 8.

Pepper Salad

2 large green peppers
2 large red peppers
6 tomatoes
6 hard-boiled eggs, sliced
1 can anchovy fillets, chopped
Herb Dressing (see index)

1. Wash peppers. Remove seeds and cut into strips.
2. Slice tomatoes thickly. Place on bottom of serving dish. Sprinkle with salad dressing.
3. Place layer of peppers on top of tomatoes, then a layer of eggs. Sprinkle with dressing after each layer. Continue until all ingredients are used.
4. Sprinkle anchovy fillets on top.

Serves 6.

Antipasto

1 lettuce	12 radishes
4 tomatoes, cut in wedges	12 black olives
1 large can tuna	1 red pepper, sliced
1 can artichoke hearts	4 stalks celery, cut in two-inch
6 slices salami	(5-cm) pieces
6 slices Prosciutto	3 tablespoons chopped parsley
6 anchovy fillets	2 tablespoons capers

1. Wash, drain and dry lettuce. Arrange leaves on a large platter.
2. Toss tomatoes in the Italian Dressing. Place on lettuce leaves.
3. Drain tuna, break into chunks and put on lettuce with the tomatoes.
4. Drain artichoke hearts and toss lightly in the dressing.
5. Arrange artichoke hearts, salami, Prosciutto, anchovy fillets, radishes, olives, pepper, celery on the platter.
6. Sprinkle with parsley, capers and Italian Dressing.

Italian Dressing:
½ cup (125 ml) olive oil
2 anchovy fillets, finely
   chopped
juice of one lemon
1 small clove of garlic,
   crushed
salt and pepper

Blend olive oil with the anchovy fillets, mashing with a fork until they are well mixed with the oil. Add lemon juice and garlic; mix thoroughly. Season to taste with salt and pepper.

Blue Cheese Mold

1 tablespoon gelatin
¼ cup cold water
2 cups (500 g) cottage cheese
½ cup (125 ml) cream

¼ lb (125 g) blue cheese
2 tablespoons chopped chives
½ lb (250 g) black olives
shredded lettuce

1. Soften gelatin in cold water and dissolve over hot water.
2. Combine cottage cheese, cream, blue cheese and chives and mix thoroughly.
3. Add the gelatin and mix well.
4. Pour into a wet mold and chill until firm.
5. Unmold onto a bed of shredded lettuce and garnish with olives.

Serves 6-8.

Chicken Salad Supreme

1 lb (500 g) cooked chicken,
  cut into bite-size pieces
¼ lb (125 g) stuffed green olives,
  sliced
1 cup chopped celery

½ cup (80 g) whole almonds
2 tablespoons chopped gherkins
3 hard-boiled eggs, chopped
  coarsely
1 cup (250 ml) mayonnaise

1. Combine the chicken, olives, celery, almonds, gherkins and eggs. Toss thoroughly.
2. Add the mayonnaise and mix well. Season to taste with salt.
3. Serve on lettuce or watercress.

Serves 6-8.

49

Cauliflower Salad

1 medium sized cauliflower
1 can anchovy fillets, chopped
¼ lb (125 g) black olives,
   pitted and sliced
½ cup chopped celery
2 scallions, chopped

1 tablespoon capers
pepper
3 tablespoons olive
   or vegetable oil
1 tablespoon vinegar

1. Wash the cauliflower and cut into small flowerets.
2. Place in saucepan and pour boiling salted water over the cauliflower and cook for 5 minutes. Drain and cool.
3. When cool, mix the cauliflower with the anchovy fillets, olives, celery, scallions and capers.
4. Mix the oil with the vinegar and peppers. Pour over the salad and mix well.
5. Chill for ½ hour before serving.

Serves 6.

Zucchini and Rice Salad

4 medium zucchini
¼ cup (105 g) rice
2 medium tomatoes

¼ lb (125 g) black olives
2 tablespoons chopped parsley
mint

1. Put the zucchini in a saucepan and cover with boiling salted water. Cook for 3 minutes or less. Drain, cool and cut into inch long pieces.
2. Boil the rice until tender. Drain and allow to dry.
3. Slice the tomatoes.
4. Pit and slice the olives.
5. Mix the zucchini with rice, tomatoes, olives and parsley.
6. Pour French Dressing or dressing of your choice over the salad. Mix gently and garnish with mint.

Serves 4-6.

Shrimp Salad in Gelatin

1 lb (500 g) cooked shrimp,
  chopped
6 hard-boiled eggs, chopped
1½ cups finely chopped celery
2 tablespoons chopped
  red pepper
1 cup (250 ml) mayonnaise
1 cup (250 ml) chili sauce
2 tablespoons capers

juice of one lemon
½ cup (125 ml) tomato sauce
½ teaspoon sugar
1 tablespoon Worcestershire
  sauce
¼ teaspoon paprika
2 tablespoons unflavored
  gelatin
½ cup (125 ml) cold water

1. In a large bowl, mix all the ingredients except the gelatin and water. Set aside.
2. Mix the water and gelatin and let it soak for five minutes. Place over hot water until dissolved.
3. Add gelatin to the shrimp and egg mixture. Blend well.
4. Pour into a ring mold and chill until firm.
5. Unmold and fill center with Mayonnaise Tarragon. (see index)

Serves 6.

Celery Slaw

2 teaspoons salt
1 tablespoon sugar
½ teaspoon pepper
pinch paprika
½ cup (125 ml) vegetable oil

3 tablespoons vinegar
½ cup (125 g) sour cream
½ bunch celery, thinly sliced
1 onion, sliced
1 medium carrot, shredded

1. Combine the salt, sugar, pepper, paprika, oil and vinegar. Beat well.
2. Add the sour cream. Beat again.
3. Pour the dressing over the celery. Chill for about three hours.
4. Before serving add the onion and carrot. Mix thoroughly.

Serves 4-6.

Chicken and Avocado Salad

1 lettuce, broken into bite-size pieces
1 bunch watercress, cut up (discard hard stems)
1 lb (500 g) cooked chicken, chopped
2 cups diced celery
4 scallions, sliced (green and white parts)

4 medium tomatoes, cut into small pieces
2 medium avocados, peeled and cubed
¼ lb (125 g) stuffed green olives, sliced

1. Combine all the ingredients.
2. Pour over Chopped Egg Dressing and toss lightly.

Serves 6-8.

Spicy Chicken Salad

1 lb (500 g) cooked chicken, diced
4 stalks celery, diced
¼ cup (62.5 ml) vegetable oil
2 tablespoons malt vinegar
juice of ½ lemon
1 hard-boiled egg, finely chopped

½ cup (125 ml) mayonnaise
½ cup (125 g) sour cream
2 tablespoons chili sauce
2 tablespoons capers
1 teaspoon salt

1. Mix chicken, celery, oil, vinegar and lemon juice.
2. Put in refrigerator and chill for several hours.
3. Mix chopped egg with mayonnaise, sour cream, chili sauce, capers and salt.
4. Pour the dressing over the chicken mixture and mix well.
5. Serve on a bed of crisp lettuce.

Serves 6.

Potato-Celery Salad

1 bunch celery
2 lb (1 kg) potatoes, cooked
4 green apples
1 clove garlic, crushed
2 egg yolks

salt and pepper
6 tablespoons olive or salad oil
2 tablespoons lemon juice
2 teaspoons chopped dill

1. Wash and drain the celery. Cut into one-inch (2½-cm) slices.
2. Cut the potatoes into small cubes.
3. Core the apples but do not peel. Cut into bite-size pieces.
4. Throughly mix the garlic and the egg yolks with the salt and pepper.
5. Gradually stir in the oil, drop by drop. Stir until mixture is thick.
6. Add the lemon juice slowly, stirring constantly.
7. Pour dressing over the celery, potatoes and apples and toss gently.
8. Garnish with chopped dill.

Serves 6-8.

Stuffed Tomatoes

6 large tomatoes
salt
pepper
4 stalks celery, chopped
3 green apples
¼ cup (62.5 ml) lemon juice

1 teaspoon brown sugar
¼ cup (62.5 ml) sour cream
¼ cup (62.5 ml) olive or salad oil
1 tablespoon prepared horseradish
chopped chives to garnish

1. Cut off top of tomatoes (stem end) and scoop out pulp. Reserve pulp.
2. Sprinkle inside of tomatoes with salt and pepper.
3. Mix the celery with the apples which have been cored and chopped but not peeled.
4. Pour lemon juice mixed with the sugar over the apples and celery and toss.
5. Combine the sour cream with the oil and horseradish sauce. Season with salt and pepper.
6. Mix thoroughly the tomato pulp, apple and celery mixture, and the sour cream dressing.
7. Fill tomato cups and sprinkle with chopped chives.

Serves 6.

Lobster and Shrimp Salad

½ cooked lobster
3 hard-boiled eggs
1 medium onion
1 green pepper
1 cup chopped celery
1 tablespoon chopped parsley
2 tablespoons olive oil

1 tablespoon vinegar
1 teaspoon prepared mustard
salt and pepper
½ lb (250 g) cooked
   shelled shrimp
lettuce
chopped dill

1. Remove the lobster meat from the shell and cut into bite-size pieces.
2. Coarsely chop the eggs, onion and pepper. Mix with the celery and parsley.
3. Mix the oil, vinegar and mustard. Season to taste with salt and pepper.
4. Combine the lobster with the egg and onion mixture. Add the shrimp and mix well.
5. Pour the dressing over the salad and toss thoroughly.
6. Spoon onto a bed of lettuce leaves and garnish with chopped dill.

Serves 4-6.

Tuna Fish and Green Bean Salad

1 lb (500 g) green beans
1 large can tuna fish
2 tablespoons chopped capers
½ cup chopped celery

1. Place beans in a saucepan and pour boiling salted water over them. Cook for three minutes. Drain.
2. Break up tuna fish and add to the green beans (left uncut), capers and celery.
3. Pour French or Vinaigrette dressing over and toss lightly.

Serves 4-6.

Hot Potato Salad

10 medium size potatoes
2 medium onions, chopped
salt and pepper
½ teaspoon celery seed
1 egg

½ lb (250 g) bacon
2 tablespoons hot bacon fat
½ cup (125 ml) hot vinegar
¼ cup (62.5 ml) hot water
2 hard-boiled eggs, chopped

1. Boil the potatoes in their skins until tender. While still hot, slice the potatoes.
2. Mix the potatoes with the onions, salt and pepper and celery seed.
3. Fry the bacon until crisp. Remove from fat. Reserve two tablespoons of the bacon fat.
4. Beat egg well. Add the warm fat, hot vinegar and hot water. Mix well.
5. Pour over the potatoes and onions.
6. Add chopped hard-boiled eggs and toss lightly.

Serves 6-8.

Marinated Mushrooms

1½ lb (750 g) mushrooms
1 cup (250 ml) vinegar
1 clove garlic, crushed
1 teaspoon salt
½ teaspoon pepper
1 bay leaf

pinch of thyme
3 scallions, chopped
¼ cup (62.5 ml) olive oil
1 tablespoon tomato sauce
2 tablespoons chopped chives
lettuce leaves

1. Clean mushrooms with a damp cloth. If large, cut in half.
2. Boil together for five minutes the vinegar, garlic, salt, pepper, bay leaf, thyme and scallions. Cool.
3. Add olive oil, tomato sauce and pour over mushrooms.
4. Allow to marinate for three hours.
5. Before serving, strain dressing and pour back over the mushrooms.
6. Serve on a bed of lettuce leaves and garnish with chopped chives.

Serves 6.

Potato and Beef Salad

¾ lb (375 g) cold cooked beef,
cut into strips
4 tomatoes, quartered
4 potatoes, cooked and diced

2 tablespoons chopped parsley
1 large dill pickle, chopped
3 tablespoons chopped chives
bunch of watercress

1. Combine the beef, tomatoes, potatoes, parsley, pickle and chives. Mix well.
2. Pour on French Dressing or a dressing of your choice. Toss thoroughly.
3. Put on a bed of watercress.

Serves 4.

Calico Salad

2 medium potatoes, cooked
and diced
3 medium carrots, diced
1 cup cooked green peas
1 red pepper, chopped

1 green pepper, chopped
1 onion, chopped
2 tablespoons chopped parsley
1 red apple, chopped with skin
½ lettuce

1. Combine all the vegetables and the apple and marinate in French Dressing for one hour.
2. Wash, drain and dry the lettuce. Cut into bite-size pieces and add the vegetables. Toss lightly.

Serves 6.

Avocado Cucumber Mold

2 packages lime gelatin
1½ cups (375 ml) boiling water
1½ cups (375 ml) cold water
1 large cucumber, diced
1 teaspoon salt
½ cup (125 ml) vinegar

2 avocados
juice of one lemon
¼ lb (125 g) stuffed green
  olives, sliced
lettuce

1. Dissolve the gelatin in the boiling water. Add the cold water and chill.
2. Marinate the cucumber in the salt and vinegar.
3. Peel and seed the avocados and cut into cubes.
4. Toss the avocados in the lemon juice and sprinkle with salt.
5. When gelatin is slightly thickened, add the drained cucumber, olives and avocado cubes. Mix lightly.
6. Pour into a wet ring mold and chill until firm.
7. Unmold onto a bed of lettuce and garnish with fresh sprigs of mint.
8. If desired, pour Cucumber Dressing over the mold.

Serves 6.

Layered Salad

1 large bunch watercress
½ Chinese cabbage, shredded
1 cucumber, sliced
6 hard-boiled eggs, halved

slices of beets, fresh or canned
2 tablespoons chopped chives
½ teaspoon marjoram
6 anchovy fillets, chopped

1. Line a salad bowl with the watercress.
2. In layers place, first the cabbage, then the cucumber, eggs and beets.
3. Sprinkle with the chopped chives and marjoram.
4. Top with the chopped anchovy fillets.
5. Pour Spicy French Dressing over the salad. See index for dressing.

Serves 6.

Orange and Date Salad

1 cup (160 g) dates (without seeds)
6 oranges
1 lettuce
French Dressing (see index)
mayonnaise

1. Slice dates and soak in French Dressing for one hour.
2. Peel the oranges and slice in rounds.
3. Wash, drain and dry the lettuce. Break up into pieces and put in salad bowl.
4. Place orange rounds on top of lettuce.
5. Drain the dates and sprinkle over oranges.
6. Pour French Dressing over it all.
7. Put dots of mayonnaise on top of salad.

Serves 6.

Banana and Chicken Salad

1 lb (500 g) cooked chicken, diced
3 bananas
juice of two lemons
½ cup mayonnaise

curry powder
lettuce
½ cup shredded coconut
3 hard-boiled eggs
paprika

1. Slice bananas and dip into lemon juice to avoid discoloring.
2. Combine chicken and bananas.
3. Mix mayonnaise with curry powder to taste.
4. Add mayonnaise to the chicken and bananas. Mix well.
5. Spoon onto lettuce.
6. Sprinkle coconut over the top.
7. Garnish with egg slices and paprika.

Serves 6-8.

Cooked Salad

½ lb (250 g) mushrooms
½ cup olive
or vegetable oil
1 green pepper
3 medium tomatoes,
quartered
½ medium cucumber,
thinly sliced

½ lb (250 g) cooked asparagus
tips
1 teaspoon salt
¼ teaspoon pepper
2 tablespoons vinegar
1 lettuce

1. Wipe the mushrooms with a damp cloth. Cut into quarters and sauté for three minutes in the oil. Remove from the oil and cool.
2. Slice the green pepper and sauté in the same oil for one minute. Remove from oil and cool.
3. Mix the tomatoes, cucumber, asparagus tips and green pepper together.
4. Season with salt and pepper and the vinegar. Mix well.
5. Wash, drain and dry the lettuce. Tear up into bite-size pieces.
6. Immediately before serving add the lettuce to the other ingredients as well as the oil used to saute the mushrooms and pepper. Toss well.

Serves 6-8.

Cheese Salad

1 lettuce
½ cup finely chopped
celery
3 tablespoons olive oil
1 tablespoon vinegar

2 teaspoons prepared mustard
1 medium onion, finely
chopped
½ lb (250 g) cheese
1 tablespoon capers

1. Wash, drain and dry the lettuce. Tear up into small pieces and put in a salad bowl.
2. Mix the oil, vinegar, mustard and onion. Beat well.
3. Shred the cheese and add to the dressing. Set aside for one hour.
4. Pour dressing on the lettuce and toss gently.
5. Garnish with capers.

Serves 6-8.

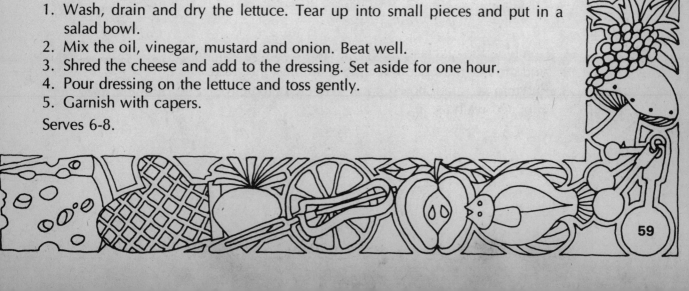

Caesar Salad

2 cloves garlic, crushed
¼ cup (125 ml) vegetable
  or olive oil
2 cups bread cubes
1 large or 2 small lettuces
can of anchovies
¼ cup (62.5 ml) vegetable
  or olive oil
½ teaspoon salt

½ teaspoon pepper
1 tablespoon Worcestershire
  sauce
¼ teaspoon dry mustard
¼ cup (125 ml) lemon juice
2 eggs boiled for 2 minutes
½ cup (107 g) Parmesan cheese,
  grated

1. Sauté bread cubes in the garlic and oil until golden brown. Set aside.
2. Tear up lettuce and put in a large salad bowl.
3. Mash anchovies with the oil, salt, pepper, Worcestershire sauce, dry mustard and lemon juice. Pour over lettuce.
4. Remove eggs from shells and beat well. Pour over the salad and toss well.
5. Sprinkle with Parmesan cheese and bread cubes. Mix thoroughly and serve immediately.

Serves 6-8.

Chicken Salad

1 lb (500 g) cooked chicken,
  diced
1 cup chopped celery
½ lb (250 g) seedless grapes
½ teaspoon salt
½ teaspoon freshly ground
  black pepper

½ cup (125 ml) mayonnaise
½ cup (125 g) sour cream
½ cup chopped walnuts

1. Combine the chicken, celery, grapes, salt and pepper.
2. Add the mayonnaise and sour cream and mix well.
3. Put into a salad bowl lined with lettuce leaves and sprinkle with the chopped walnuts.

Serves 4-6.

Potato Salad

4 lb (2 kg) potatoes
½ cup (125 ml) vinegar
1 onion, chopped
½ cup (125 ml) water
½ cup (125 ml) salad oil
2 onions, sliced

½ cup (125 g) sour cream
salt and pepper
minced parsley
2 hard-boiled eggs,
 riced

1. Boil potatoes in their skins until tender. While still warm, slice thinly.
2. Put vinegar, chopped onion and water in a small saucepan and bring to a boil. Remove from heat.
3. In a large salad bowl put a layer of potatoes and then a layer of sliced onions. Sprinkle salt, pepper, a little oil and a few spoonfuls of the vinegar mixture over the potatoes and onions. Continue the layering until the potatoes and onion are used.
4. Gently fold in the sour cream.
5. Garnish with parsley and riced eggs.

Serves 8-10.

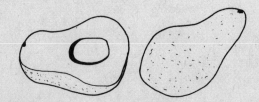

Avocado and Strawberry Salad

2 tablespoons gelatin
¼ cup (62.5 ml) cold water
1½ cups (375 ml) water
1 cup (330 g) currant jam
juice of 2 oranges

juice of 2 lemons
¼ cup sugar
4 avocados
1 pint strawberries

1. Soak the gelatin in the cold water.
2. Boil the 1½ cups water, jam, juices and sugar for five minutes.
3. Dissolve the gelatin in the hot liquid and let it cool.
4. Cut the avocados in half and remove the seeds.
5. Fill the avocados with whole strawberries.
6. Pour cooled gelatin mixture over the strawberries and chill until firm.

Serves 8.

Fennel and Cucumber Salad

2 oranges
1 cucumber
1 fennel root
10 radishes
½ cup chopped mint
3 tablespoons olive
   or vegetable oil

2 tablespoons lemon juice
1 clove garlic, crushed
½ teaspoon dry mustard
pinch of sugar
3 hard-boiled eggs

1. Peel the oranges and divide into segments.
2. Wash the cucumber (do not peel) and cut into chunks.
3. Cut the fennel into thin strips.
4. Slice the radishes thinly.
5. Mix all the vegetables together and add half of the chopped mint.
6. Blend the oil, lemon juice, garlic, mustard and sugar.
7. Pour the dressing over the salad and toss lightly.
8. Garnish with hard-boiled eggs cut into quarters and the remaining mint.

Serves 4-6.

Eggplant and Ham Salad

3 small eggplants
½ cup (125 ml) olive oil
1 clove garlic, crushed
4 tablespoons chopped parsley
½ lb (250 g) ham, diced

2 red peppers
3 tablespoons vegetable oil
1 tablespoon lemon juice
salt and pepper

1. Dice the eggplants (do not peel) and sauté gently in the olive oil.
2. Add the garlic and the parsley. Mix well but carefully.
3. Add the ham and the peppers which have been chopped to the eggplant mixture.
4. Mix the oil, lemon juice, salt and pepper and pour over the salad.
5. Toss gently and chill.

Serves 4-6.

Potato Salad with Fish

1 lb (500 g) cooked fish
 fillets
1 lb (500 g) cooked diced
 potatoes
½ cup celery, chopped
½ onion, chopped

3 tablespoons chopped parsley
1 tablespoon chopped chives
French Dressing (see index)
salt and pepper
paprika

1. Break the fish into bite-size pieces.
2. Combine the fish with the potatoes, celery, onion, parsley and chives. Mix well.
3. Add the dressing and toss thoroughly.
4. Season to taste with salt and pepper.
5. Garnish with paprika.

Serves 4-6.

Fruit Salad

1 avocado
2 tablespoons lemon juice
½ cantaloupe
1 cup pineapple cubes
1 punnet strawberries
1 red apple, diced with skin

lettuce leaves
1 lb (500 g) cottage cheese
½ cup (125 ml) mayonnaise
1 tablespoon honey
2 tablespoons (20 g)
 chopped walnuts

1. Peel the avocado and cut it into strips. Dip in lemon juice to avoid discoloring.
2. Gently mix the fruits together.
3. Spoon cottage cheese onto lettuce leaves.
4. Put fruit on top.
5. Mix the mayonnaise with the honey and walnuts.
6. Pour dressing over the fruit.
7. Garnish with avocado slices.

Serves 4-6.

Tomato and Herb Salad

1 tablespoon chopped thyme
1 tablespoon chopped tarragon
1 tablespoon chopped marjoram
1 tablespoon chopped chives

1 tablespoon chopped basil
6 medium tomatoes
½ cup (82 g) raisins

1. Mix the herbs together.
2. Quarter the tomatoes.
3. Chop the raisins.
4. Mix the tomatoes and raisins.
5. Sprinkle with the chopped herbs.
6. Pour French Dressing over it all (or use a dressing of your choice) and chill well.

Serves 4.

Broccoli Salad

1 lb (500 g) broccoli heads
2 tablespoons olive
  or vegetable oil
1 tablespoon vinegar
2 tablespoons chopped parsley

1 tablespoon chopped capers
3 tablespoons mayonnaise
1 tablespoon lemon juice
lettuce
cayenne

1. Put the broccoli in a saucepan and cover with boiling salted water. Cook for 10 minutes. Drain and cool.
2. When cool sprinkle oil and vinegar over the broccoli and chill for one hour.
3. Combine parsley, capers, mayonnaise and lemon juice.
4. Pour dressing over the broccoli.
5. Arrange on lettuce leaves.
6. Sprinkle cayenne for color.

Serves 4.

Salad Nicoise

1 lb (500 g) tomatoes
1 medium cucumber
salt and pepper
1 teaspoon basil
1 tablespoon chopped parsley

grated rind of one lemon
½ lb (250 g) green beans
½ cup (75 g) black olives
1 can anchovy fillets

1. Plunge the tomatoes in boiling water for 30 seconds. Remove from the boiling water, peel and slice.
2. Wash and slice the cucumber.
3. Lay the tomatoes and cucumber on a dish, season well with salt and pepper.
4. Sprinkle the basil, chopped parsley and grated lemon rind over it all.
5. Put prepared green beans in a saucepan and pour boiling water over them. Boil for five minutes. Drain and cool.
6. Place beans over the tomatoes and cucumber.
7. Scatter olives over the salad.
8. Pour French Dressing over it all.
9. Lay the anchovy fillets on the top.
(Canned tuna fish may also be added to the salad.)

Serves 4-6.

Leek Salad

6 leeks
1 cup chopped celery
1 tablespoon capers
salt and pepper

1. Wash leeks and cook in salted boiling water for 10 minutes.
2. Drain and chill.
3. Mix with celery and capers.
4. Serve with dressing of your choice.

Serves 4-6.

Anchovy Salad

1 large garlic clove	juice of one orange
2 small cans anchovies	1 lettuce
2 scallions, minced	1 cucumber, sliced with skin
2 tablespoons chopped parsley	3 tomatoes, quartered
tarragon vinegar	2 stalks celery, chopped
Worcestershire sauce	1 bunch radishes, sliced
2 cups (500 ml) mayonnaise	3 hard-boiled eggs, sliced

1. Rub the salad bowl with the garlic.
2. Drain one can of anchovies and mash them with the scallions.
3. Add the parsley, a little vinegar and a little Worcestershire Sauce. Mix well.
4. Add the mayonnaise and the orange juice and beat well. If the dressing is too thick add a little more vinegar and orange juice.
5. Wash, drain and dry the lettuce. Tear into bite-size pieces and put in salad bowl along with the cucumber, tomatoes, celery and radishes.
6. Pour on dressing and toss until well mixed.
7. Garnish with egg slices and anchovies from second can.

Serves 6-8.

Avocado and Egg Salad

1 clove garlic, cut	1 lettuce
¼ lb (125 g) blue cheese, crumbled	½ cup chopped celery
	3 hard-boiled eggs, sliced
2 avocados, cut in Julienne strips	French Dressing (see index)

1. Rub the salad bowl with the cut garlic.
2. Wash, drain and dry the lettuce and tear into bite-size pieces.
3. Combine the cheese, avocados, lettuce, celery and eggs in the bowl.
4. Pour French Dressing (or dressing of your choice) over the salad and mix thoroughly.

Serves 6.

Continental Salad

1 large lettuce
2 cans artichokes hearts,
quartered
2 avocados, sliced

2 cans hearts of palm,
quartered
6 hard-boiled eggs, sliced
French Dressing (see index)

1. Wash and drain the lettuce. Tear up into small pieces.
2. Add artichoke hearts, avocados and hearts of palm and toss lightly.
3. Pour French Dressing over the salad and mix carefully.
4. Lay eggs on the top and sprinkle with paprika or cayenne.

Serves 6.

Hearts of Palm Salad

2 lettuces
2 avocados
2 grapefruits, sectioned

2 tablespoons lemon juice
2 cans hearts of palm

1. Wash and drain the lettuce. Tear into bite-size pieces.
2. Peel the avocados and dice.
3. Toss the avocados in the lemon juice.
4. Place all the ingredients in a bowl, pour dressing of your choice over all and toss lightly.

Serves 8.

Asparagus Vinaigrette

4 bunches fresh asparagus
2 teaspoons salt
½ cup (125 ml) olive
or vegetable oil
4 tablespoons chopped parsley
2 hard-boiled eggs,
chopped finely

¼ cup (62.5 ml) vinegar
2 tablespoons chopped green
pepper
1 tablespoon chopped chives
pepper and paprika to taste

1. Cook the asparagus, drain and chill.
2. Mix all the remaining ingredients and beat with a rotary beater. Chill.
3. Pour sauce over the asparagus and serve.

Serves 8.

Tomato Salad Mold

1   15½ oz (445 g) can
     condensed tomato soup
1½ tablespoons gelatin
½   cup cold water
½   lb (250 g) cream cheese
1   cup (250 ml) mayonnaise

1   cup chopped celery
1   green pepper, chopped
½   onion, chopped
2   tablespoons minced parsley
½   cup (60 g) chopped walnuts

1. Heat tomato soup.
2. Soften gelatin in the cold water and add to the soup. Mix well and cool.
3. Cream together the cream cheese and the mayonnaise.
4. Add the celery, pepper, onion, parsley and walnuts to the cream cheese mixture and mix thoroughly.
5. Add to the gelatin mixture.
6. Pour into a wet mold and chill until firm.
7. Unmold onto a bed of lettuce leaves.

Serves 6-8.

Chili-Cheese Mold

1   tablespoon gelatin
¼   cup cold water
1   cup (250 g) chili sauce
1   cup (250 g) cottage cheese
½   cup (125 ml) mayonnaise

½   teaspoon salt
1   cup (250 g) cream, whipped
1   lb (500 g) tomatoes
2   tablespoons chopped chives

1. Soften gelatin in cold water. Dissolve over hot water.
2. Combine chili sauce, cottage cheese, mayonnaise and salt.
3. Add gelatin to the mixture. Mix well.
4. Fold in whipped cream.
5. Pour into a wet mold and chill until firm.
6. Unmold onto a bed of lettuce leaves.
7. Garnish with wedges of tomatoes and sprinkle with chopped chives.

Serves 6.

Cucumber and Cherry Salad

2 cucumbers
1 lb (500 g) cherries
1 cup chopped celery
lettuce
French Dressing (see index)

1. Peel the cucumbers and cut into chunks.
2. Wash and pit the cherries.
3. Combine cucumbers, cherries and celery.
4. Pour French Dressing over it all and toss well.
5. Serve in cups of lettuce leaves.
(Delicious served on top of cottage cheese.)
Serves 6.

Tomato and Black Olive Salad

6 medium tomatoes
1 clove garlic, crushed
½ cup (125 ml) mayonnaise

1 tablespoon lemon juice
salt and black pepper
¼ lb (125 g) black olives

1. Peel the tomatoes. Cut off the top and remove seeds and pulp.
2. Put the pulp into a bowl with the crushed garlic, mayonnaise and lemon juice.
3. Season to taste with salt and pepper.
4. Fill the tomatoes with this mixture.
5. Stone and coarsely chop the black olives.
6. Sprinkle over the tomatoes.
Serves 6.

Wilted Spinach Salad

½ lb (250 g) bacon
½ cup (125 ml) vinegar
½ teaspoon salt
2 teaspoons sugar
½ teaspoon mustard

¼ teaspoon pepper
1 bunch spinach
1 tablespoon chopped chives
2 teaspoons chopped dill
3 hard-boiled eggs, sliced

1. Sauté the bacon until crisp. Remove from pan.
2. Add vinegar, salt, sugar, mustard and pepper to the bacon fat and simmer for two minutes.
3. Wash the spinach, drain and dry. Tear into bite-size pieces.
4. Put spinach in salad bowl and pour vinegar and bacon fat mixture over it.
5. Add chopped chives, dill, eggs and broken up bacon.
6. Toss well and serve immediately.

Serves 6-8.

Seafood and Salad Mold

2 tablespoons gelatin
½ cup (125 ml) cold water
1 cup (250 ml) chili sauce
1½ cups (375 ml) mayonnaise
6 hard-boiled eggs, diced
1 cup chopped celery
1 red pepper, chopped

½ teaspoon sugar
dash of Tabasco sauce
1 teaspoon Worcestershire sauce
½ cup (125 ml) tomato sauce
1 lb (500 g) seafood (shrimp, crabmeat or lobster) cooked and peeled

1. Soak the gelatin in cold water. Place over hot water until dissolved.
2. Mix the remaining ingredients (excepting the seafood) and add the gelatin.
3. Pour into a wet ring mold and chill until firm.
4. When firm, unmold onto a bed of lettuce and fill the center with seafood.
5. Pour Russian Dressing (see index) over it all.

Serves 6-8.

Cucumber Salad

3 large cucumbers
1 tablespoons salt
juice of one lemon
½ cup (125 g) sour cream

2 teaspoons chopped dill
2 teaspoons chopped parsley
salt and pepper

1. Peel the cucumbers and slice very thinly.
2. Sprinkle them with the salt, put in a bowl with a weighted plate on top and leave for several hours or overnight. Pour off the liquid and dry the cucumbers.
3. Mix lemon juice, sour cream, dill and parsley. Season to taste with salt and pepper.
4. Pour Sour Cream Dressing over the cucumbers and mix thoroughly.

Serves 4-6.

Potato and Gherkin Salad

2 lb (1 kg) cooked potatoes
4 tablespoons chopped gherkins
2 tablespoons cocktail onions
1 tablespoon capers
2 tablespoons olive
   or vegetable oil

1 tablespoon vinegar
2 teaspoons prepared mustard
salt, pepper and sugar
chopped parsley and dill

1. Slice the potatoes and mix the gherkins, onion and capers.
2. Blend the oil, vinegar and mustard. Season to taste with salt, pepper and sugar.
3. Pour the dressing over the potatoes and gherkins and toss well.
4. Allow the salad to marinate for at least two hours before serving.

Serves 6.

Blue Cheese Salad

1 lettuce
½ lb (250 g) beets,
 cut in strips
¼ lb (125 g) blue cheese
1 cup chopped celery
French Dressing (see index)

1. Wash and drain the lettuce. Tear into bite-size pieces.
2. Mix beets, blue cheese and celery. Chill.
3. Just before serving, pour French Dressing (or dressing of your choice) over the salad and serve immediately.

Serves 4-6.

Three-Bean Salad

1 large can green beans
1 large can wax beans
1 large can red kidney beans
1 green pepper, minced
1 onion, chopped finely
½ cup (125 ml) olive
 or vegetable oil

¼ cup (62.5 ml) malt vinegar
¼ cup (62.5 ml) white vinegar
½ cup sugar
1 teaspoon salt
½ teaspoon pepper

1. Rinse beans under running water. Drain well.
2. Combine beans with green pepper and onions. Mix well.
3. Mix oil, vinegars, sugar, salt and pepper.
4. Pour over the bean mixture. Toss well. Cover and chill until ready to serve.

Serves 8.

Day-After-Thanksgiving Salad

1 lb (500 g) cold cooked turkey
4 stalks celery, sliced
4 scallions, chopped
½ cup (62.5 g) chopped nuts
½ red or green pepper,
   chopped finely

½ cup (125 ml) mayonnaise
1 tablespoon lemon juice
salt and pepper

1. Dice the turkey into bite-size pieces.
2. Combine with the celery, scallions, nuts and pepper.
3. Blend the mayonnaise and lemon juice. Season to taste with salt and pepper.
4. Add the mayonnaise to the turkey mixture and mix thoroughly.

Serves 4.

Egg Salad

6 hard-boiled eggs
½ bunch celery, chopped
   (reserve leaves for garnishing)
5 medium carrots, grated
6 radishes, sliced
½ cucumber, diced
1 cup (250 g) plain yoghurt

1 teaspoon paprika
1 teaspoon sugar
juice of ½ lemon
1 tablespoon orange juice
1 tablespoon chopped parsley
salt and pepper

1. Quarter the eggs.
2. Gently mix them with the celery, carrots, radishes and cucumber.
3. Make the dressing by mixing the yoghurt with the paprika, sugar, lemon juice, orange juice and parsley. Season to taste with salt and pepper.
4. Pour dressing over the egg salad and toss lightly.
5. Chill and serve.

Serves 4-6.

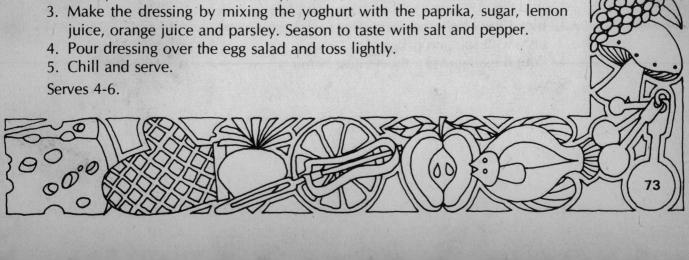

Beet and Ham Salad

1 lb (500 g) cooked, diced beets	1 lb (500 g) diced ham
½ lb (250 g) cooked, diced potatoes	½ lb (250 g) shredded Swiss cheese
French Dressing (see index)	½ cup chopped cucumber

1. Combine the beets and potatoes. Pour a little French Dressing over the mixture and toss well. Allow to marinate for one hour.
2. Add the ham, Swiss cheese and cucumber to the beets and potato mixture. Mix well.
3. Serve on a bed of lettuce leaves.

Serves 6-8.

Hot Cole Slaw

1 cucumber, peeled and sliced	3 tablespoons chopped parsley
1 small onion, grated	1½ cups (375 ml) chili sauce
1 medium cabbage, finely shredded	1¼ cups (300 ml) cream
1 green pepper, chopped	juice of one lemon
	1 tablespoon minced chives
	salt and pepper

1. Soak the cucumber in salted ice water for ½ hour. Drain and pat dry.
2. Add the cucumber to the onion, cabbage, pepper and parsley. Mix well.
3. Blend the chili sauce with the cream, lemon juice and chives. Season to taste with salt and pepper.
4. Pour dressing over cabbage just before serving and toss thoroughly.

Serves 8-10.

Green Beans and Cucumber Salad

1½ lb (750 g) green beans,
cut into one-inch pieces
½ cup water, salted and
boiling
2½ cups (625 g) sour cream
2 tablespoons chopped fresh
dill weed

½ teaspoon salt
¼ teaspoon pepper
2 tablespoons lemon juice
2 large cucumbers, sliced
very thinly

1. Pour boiling, salted water over beans and cook for five minutes, tossing occasionally. Drain and chill.
2. Mix the sour cream with the dill, salt, pepper and lemon juice and allow to stand for a couple of hours.
3. Blend the dressing with the beans and cucumbers. Chill for at least three hours.

Serves 6.

Guacamole Salad

3 avocados, peeled and sliced
3 tomatoes, chopped
juice of two lemons
chili powder
¼ lb (125 g) bacon

1. Put avocados on a bed of lettuce.
2. Sprinkle with tomatoes, lemon juice and chili powder.
3. Cook bacon in a frypan until brown and crispy. Break up into small bits.
4. Sprinkle bacon on top of avocados and pour French Dressing (see index) over it all.

Serves 6.

Chinese Salad

1 lb (500 g) bean sprouts
1 cup chopped celery
1 cucumber, sliced
1 green pepper, chopped
2 tomatoes, cut into small pieces
3 scallions, chopped
French Dressing (see index)
2 tablespoons chopped chives

1. Rinse and drain the bean sprouts.
2. Combine the bean sprouts with the celery, cucumber, pepper, tomatoes and scallions.
3. Toss with French Dressing to which has been added a teaspoon of soy sauce.
4. Chill the salad for one hour.
5. Drain off any excess dressing and sprinkle with chopped chives.

Serves 6.

Pepper, Cucumber and Radish Salad

3 cucumbers
1 green pepper
1 red pepper
1 bunch radishes
lettuce
French Dressing (see index)

1. Peel the cucumbers and slice very thinly. Soak in salted ice water for one hour. Drain and pat dry.
2. Place lettuce on a platter and arrange cucumbers on top.
3. Slice pepper in rounds. Slice radishes very thinly and lay both the peppers and the radishes on top of the cucumbers.
4. Sprinkle French dressing or the dressing of your choice over the salad and allow to stand for about fifteen minutes before serving.

Serves 6-8.

Tuna and Rice Salad

1 cup (210 g) rice
2 medium tomatoes
large can of tuna
4 tablespoons chopped chives
½ cup (125 ml) cream, whipped
½ cup (125 ml) mayonnaise

1 teaspoon celery seeds
1 tablespoon grated lemon
  rind
salt and pepper
radishes

1. Cook the rice in boiling water until tender. Drain and cook.
2. Put the tomatoes in boiling water for 30 seconds. Remove from water and peel. Chop into small pieces.
3. Drain the tuna and break into pieces.
4. Add the tuna to the rice, tomatoes and chives and mix well.
5. Fold the whipped cream into the mayonnaise. Add the celery seeds, lemon rind and salt and pepper to taste.
6. Gently mix mayonnaise mixture with the tuna and rice.
7. Press into a ring mold and refrigerate.
8. When set, unmold and garnish with radishes.

Serves 4-6.

Chicken with Almond Salad

1 cup (165 g) raisins
1 cup (160 g) whole blanched
  almonds
1 lb (500 g) cold cooked chicken
½ cup (125 g) sour cream
½ cup (125 ml) mayonnaise

1 teaspoon lemon juice
½ small onion, grated
1 tablespoon chopped parsley
lettuce

1. Soak raisins in hot water for ten minutes. Drain.
2. Cut the chicken into bite-size pieces.
3. Mix the sour cream, mayonnaise, salt, pepper and lemon juice. Chill.
4. Combine the drained raisins, almonds, chicken, grated onion and parsley.
5. Pour the mayonnaise and sour cream mixture over it all and mix well.
6. Serve in a bowl lined with lettuce leaves.

Serves 4-6.

Hearty Salad

¼ lb (125 g) green beans
2 carrots, cut in Julienne strips
1 cup chopped celery
¼ cup (62.5 ml) French Dressing (see index)
1 lettuce
¼ lb (125 g) cooked beef, cut in strips

¼ lb (125 g) ham, cut in strips
3 hard-boiled eggs
½ cup (125 ml) mayonnaise
1 tablespoon prepared horseradish sauce

1. Cook beans in salted boiling water for 3-5 minutes. Cool.
2. Add beans to carrots and celery and marinate in French Dressing for one to two hours.
3. Wash, drain and dry the lettuce. Break into bite-size pieces and put in a salad bowl.
4. Place meat on top and spoon vegetables over the meat.
5. Cut eggs in half and arrange over top of salad.
6. In center, place mayonnaise mixed with horseradish.

Serves 6.

Tomato-Egg Cups

6 large tomatoes
¼ lb (125 g) cream cheese
½ medium onion, chopped
1 medium green pepper, chopped
½ cucumber, chopped

2 tablespoons chopped parsley
1 tablespoon chopped chives
4 hard-boiled eggs
1 cup Sour Cream Dressing (see index)

1. Cut slices from top of tomatoes and scoop out centers. Sprinkle with salt. Turn upside down and chill. Reserve pulp.
2. Soften cream cheese with a little milk. Put in bottom of tomato cups.
3. Combine tomato pulp, onion, pepper, cucumber, parsley, chives, coarsely chopped eggs and ½ cup dressing.
4. Fill cups with mixture.
5. Spoon remaining dressing over top of each tomato cup.

Serves 6.

Chicken Curry Salad

1 cup (250 ml) cream, whipped
1 cup (250 ml) mayonnaise
curry powder to taste
salt and pepper
2 lb (1 kg) cooked chicken,
  diced

1½ cups chopped celery
2 red apples, cored
  and chopped
½ onion, minced
½ cucumber, chopped

1. Blend together the whipped cream and the mayonnaise. Add the curry powder, salt and pepper to taste.
2. Combine the chicken, celery, apples, onion and cucumber.
3. Mix in the dressing and chill well.

Serves 8.

White Salad with Sour Cream Dressing

1 small cauliflower
2 stalks celery
1 onion
1 cucumber

salt and pepper
white vinegar
parsley
paprika

1. Wash the cauliflower and cut into flowerets. Chop the celery. Cut the onion into rings. Slice the cucumber.
2. Arrange all the vegetables on a platter. Sprinkle salt, pepper, vinegar, parsley and paprika.
3. Serve with Sour Cream Dressing.

Sour Cream Dressing:

Combine 1¼ cups (300 g) sour cream with 2 tablespoons lemon juice, ½ teaspoon salt and a dash of cayenne pepper. Mix well.

Serves 6.

Cheesy Pear Salad

4 fresh pears, peeled and diced
2 cups (250 g) grated cheddar cheese
1 cup (250 ml) mayonnaise
2 tablespoons chopped mint
3 teaspoons chopped chives
lettuce leaves

1. Toss the pears with the cheese.
2. Mix together the mayonnaise, mint and chives.
3. Combine with the pears and cheese.
4. Serve on a bed of lettuce leaves.

Serves 4.

Nutty Salad

2 cups (500 ml) cream
2 eggs, beaten
2 medium carrots, finely chopped
1½ tablespoons honey
½ teaspoon salt
2 stalks celery, chopped
1 green pepper, chopped
2 tablespoons chopped parsley
1 tablespoon chopped chives
1 cup (120 g) chopped walnuts
lettuce leaves

1. Scald the cream and pour over the beaten eggs. Mix well. Cook over a low heat for about two minutes.
2. Add the carrots, honey and salt and cook for another two minutes.
3. Add celery, green pepper, parsley, chives and nuts and mix thoroughly. Chill.
4. Serve on lettuce leaves.

Serves 2-4.

Banana-Pineapple Salad

4 bananas
¼ cup (62.5 ml) lemon juice
1 pineapple, diced
¼ cup (62.5 ml) salad oil
lettuce leaves
chopped parsley

1. Peel and slice the bananas and toss in lemon juice.
2. Combine the bananas with the pineapple.
3. Add the oil and mix well.
4. Serve on lettuce leaves and sprinkle with chopped parsley.

Serves 4.

Chicken and Asparagus Salad

1 can asparagus, cut up	4 tablespoons mayonnaise
1 lb (500 g) cooked chicken	salt and pepper
2 red apples	1 teaspoon prepared mustard
2 tablespoons lemon juice	2 tablespoons chopped parsley
¼ lb (125 g) cottage cheese	1 tablespoon chopped chives

1. Drain the asparagus. Dice the chicken and chop the unpeeled apples.
2. Combine the lemon juice, cottage cheese, mayonnaise, salt and pepper to taste. Add mustard, parsley and chives and mix well.
3. Mix the asparagus, chicken and apples with the cottage cheese mixture. Chill for several hours.

Serves 4-6.

Winter Salad

½ lb (250 g) tomatoes
2 onions
2 carrots
¼ white cabbage
½ green pepper
Italian Dressing
  (see index)

1. Wash and thinly slice the tomatoes.
2. Grate the onions and carrots.
3. Shred the cabbage finely.
4. Slice the pepper thinly.
5. Mix all the vegetables and toss lightly in Italian Dressing.

Serves 4-6.

Mushroom and Watercress Salad

1 lettuce
½ cabbage
½ lb (250 g) button mushrooms
1 cup (125 g) grated cheddar cheese

1 bunch watercress
2 tablespoons chopped parsley
Herb Dressing

1. Wash, drain and dry the lettuce. Tear into bite-size pieces.
2. Shred the cabbage.
3. Slice the mushrooms and combine with the cheese and prepared watercress.
4. Combine all ingredients and toss in Herb Dressing.

Serves 4-6.

Banana-Nut Salad

4 bananas, peeled and sliced
¼ cup (62.5 ml) lemon juice
1 cup (120 g) chopped walnuts

½ cup (125 ml) mayonnaise
2 tablespoons parsley, chopped
lettuce leaves

1. Toss the sliced bananas in the lemon juice.
2. Add the walnuts to the bananas.
3. Mix the mayonnaise with the parsley and add to the bananas and walnuts.
4. Serve on a bed of lettuce leaves.

Serves 4.

Tomato and Lima Bean Salad

4 tomatoes, quartered
1 cup cooked lima beans
½ cup (125 g) plain yoghurt

½ cup (125 ml) mayonnaise
1 teaspoon salt
¼ teaspoon black pepper

1. Combine the tomatoes and lima beans.
2. Mix the yoghurt with the mayonnaise. Season with salt and pepper.
3. Add to the tomatoes and lima beans and mix thoroughly.

Serves 4.

Salad Dressings

Cole Slaw Dressing

  1 cup (250 ml) mayonnaise
  2 tablespoons vinegar
  2 tablespoons prepared mustard
  ½ cup (125 ml) cream
  1 teaspoon salt
  ¼ teaspoon pepper

Combine all ingredients. Mix well.

Thousand Island Dressing

  1 cup (250 ml) mayonnaise
  ½ cup (125 ml) chili sauce
  2 hard-boiled eggs, chopped
     finely
  1 teaspoon Worcestershire sauce
  ¼ cup chopped celery
  1 teaspoon paprika
  ¼ cup sweet pickle relish
  ¼ green pepper, chopped finely
  ½ onion, grated

Combine all ingredients. Mix thoroughly. Chill.

Sour Cream Dressing

1 cup (250 g) sour cream
½ cup (125 ml) mayonnaise
2 teaspoons lemon juice
1 tablespoon prepared
   horseradish sauce
pinch of cayenne
salt and paprika to taste
¼ teaspoon dry mustard.

Combine all ingredients and mix thoroughly.

White Wine Dressing

½ cup (125 ml) olive oil
¼ cup (62.5 ml) dry white wine
2 teaspoons lemon juice
1 teaspoon salt
¼ teaspoon freshly ground
   black pepper
¼ teaspoon dry mustard
¼ teaspoon sugar
½ teaspoon minced onion
pinch of cayenne

Mix together all ingredients and chill.

Cream Dressing

1 tablespoon dry mustard
1 teaspoon salt
2 teaspoons flour
1½ teaspoons confectioners' sugar
pinch cayenne

½ cup (125 ml) vinegar
1 egg yolk
1 tablespoon (20 g) butter
  or margarine, melted
1 cup (250 ml) cream, whipped

Mix dry ingredients together in the top of a double boiler. Slowly add the vinegar, egg yolk and butter. Cook over boiling water until mixture thickens. Remove from boiling water and cool. When cool, add whipped cream.

Honey Dressing

½ cup sugar
1 teaspoon dry mustard
1 teaspoon paprika
¼ teaspoon salt
½ cup honey

¼ cup (62.5 ml) vinegar
2 tablespoons lemon juice
1 teaspoon grated onion
1 cup (250 ml) salad oil

Mix dry ingredients. Add honey, vinegar, lemon juice and onion. Pour oil into mixture very slowly, beating constantly with rotary or electric beater.

Cooked Dressing

4 tablespoons sugar
2 teaspoons salt
4 tablespoons flour
2 teaspoons dry mustard
pinch of cayenne

4 lightly beaten egg yolks
1½ cup (375 ml) milk
½ cup (125 ml) vinegar
1 tablespoon (20 g) butter
  or margarine

Mix the dry ingredients. Add the egg yolks and milk and cook in a double boiler over boiling water until the mixture is thick, stirring constantly. Add vinegar and butter, mix well and cool.

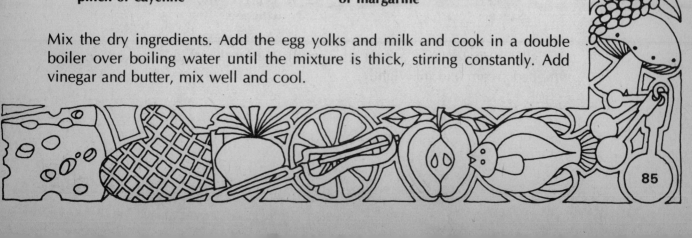

Herb Dressing

1½ cups (375 ml) mayonnaise	2 tablespoons vinegar
1½ teaspoons prepared mustard	1½ teaspoons ground marjoram
½ teaspoon Tabasco sauce	½ teaspoon ground thyme
chili powder to taste	1 clove garlic, crushed

Put all ingredients in a screw top jar and shake well until blended.

Cucumber Dressing

1 cup (250 ml) sour cream	½ teaspoon salt
juice of one lemon	2 teaspoons minced onion
1 teaspoon prepared mustard	1 cup finely chopped cucumber
½ teaspoon dill seed	

Combine all ingredients and blend thoroughly.

Mayonnaise Tarragon

1 cup (250 ml) mayonnaise	1 teaspoon tomato sauce
½ teaspoon paprika	1 tablespoon tarragon vinegar
½ teaspoon Worcestershire Sauce	½ cup (125 ml) cream, whipped

Mix all the ingredients except the cream. When thoroughly mixed add the whipped cream and mix lightly.

Lemon Dressing

4 tablespoons lemon juice
½ teaspoon sugar
¼ teaspoon salt
pinch of pepper
4 tablespoons olive
    or salad oil

Dissolve sugar in lemon juice. Combine with the remaining ingredients and mix thoroughly.

Blue Cheese Dressing

¼ lb (125 g) blue cheese
½ cup (125 ml) olive oil
¼ teaspoon paprika
1 tablespoon lemon juice
1 tablespoon vinegar

2 teaspoons Worcestershire
    sauce
½ teaspoon dry mustard
1 teaspoon brandy
salt to taste

Rub cheese through a sieve. Slowly mix with the oil. Add remaining ingredients and mix until well blended and smooth.

Chopped Egg Dressing

1 cup (250 ml) olive oil
1 cup (250 ml) vinegar
2 tablespoons chopped chives
6 hard-boiled eggs, chopped
    finely

1 cup (250 ml) mayonnaise
1 clove crushed garlic

Combine olive oil and vinegar. Add remaining ingredients and blend thoroughly.

Hot French Dressing

1 cup (250 ml) salad oil
¼ cup (62.5 g) sugar
½ cup (125 ml) tomato sauce
½ cup (125 ml) Worcestershire sauce

½ cup (125 ml) vinegar
½ teaspoon salt
¼ teaspoon freshly ground black pepper

Combine all ingredients in a saucepan. Bring to a boil and serve hot.

Lorenzo Dressing

1 cup (250 ml) olive or salad oil
½ cup (125 ml) vinegar
1 teaspoon salt

paprika
½ cup (125 ml) chili sauce
1 cup chopped watercress

Combine all ingredients and mix thoroughly. Chill.

Green Goddess Dressing

1 small can anchovies, chopped
3 tablespoons chopped chives
1 tablespoon lemon juice
3 tablespoons tarragon vinegar
1 cup (250 g) sour cream

1 cup (250 ml) mayonnaise
½ cup chopped parsley
pinch freshly ground black pepper
½ teaspoon salt

Combine all ingredients in an electric blender and mix for 30 seconds. Chill.

Italian Dressing

1 cup (250 ml) olive oil
4 anchovy fillets, finely chopped
¼ cup (62.5 ml) lemon juice
salt and freshly ground
    black pepper to taste

1 tablespoon capers, finely
    chopped

Combine all ingredients and mix well. Chill.

Summer Dressing

1 cup (250 ml) French Dressing
1 hard-boiled egg, finely
    chopped
1 tablespoon minced parsley
1 tablespoon chopped green
    pepper

2 tablespoons cooked minced
    beets
2 teaspoons chopped chives

Combine ingredients and beat well.

Cream Cheese Dressing

¼ lb (125 g) cream cheese
1 tablespoon lemon juice
3 tablespoons currant jam
    or jelly
1 cup (250 ml) cream, whipped

Blend the cream cheese with the lemon juice and jam. Add the cream and mix thoroughly.

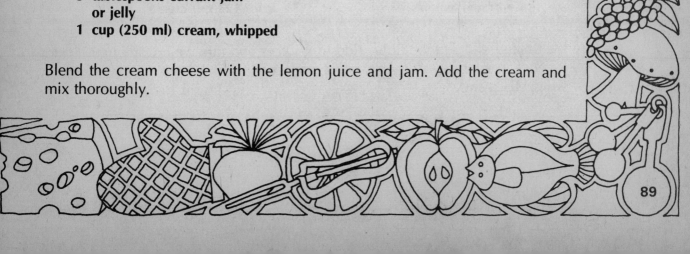

Mayonnaise

1 teaspoon mustard	3 egg yolks
1 teaspoon salt	3 tablespoons vinegar
1 teaspoon icing sugar	2 cups (500 ml) olive oil
pinch of cayenne	3 tablespoons lemon juice

Mix dry ingredients, add egg yolks and mix well. Add half a teaspoon vinegar. Slowly add the oil: at first drop by drop, beating constantly. Add vinegar and lemon juice as the mixture thickens.

Variations of mayonnaise

Celery dressing: Combine 1 cup (250 ml) mayonnaise with one tablespoon chopped green pepper, 1 tablespoon minced parsley, 1 cup chopped celery, 2 tablespoons lemon juice, ¼ teaspoon each of salt and paprika.

Creamy dressing: To one cup of mayonnaise add one cup of whipped cream.

Savory dressing: To one cup of mayonnaise add 1 teaspoon prepared mustard, 1 teaspoon Worcestershire sauce and 2 teaspoons grated onion.

Fruit Mayonnaise

1 tablespoon (20 g) butter	juice of one orange
2 tablespoons flour	1 teaspoon grated orange and
1½ cups (375 ml) grapefruit or	lemon rind
pineapple juice	2 eggs, separated
juice of one lemon	½ cup (125 ml) cream

Melt butter and add the flour. Add fruit juices and mix well. Cook until thick. Remove from heat. Add egg yolks and cool. Add beaten egg whites and whipped cream.

Fruit Dressing

½ cup sugar
2 teaspoons flour
1 egg yolk
juice of one lemon

½ cup (125 ml) unsweetened
  pineapple juice
1 cup (250 ml) cream,
  whipped

Combine sugar, flour and egg yolk and mix well. Add pineapple and lemon juices. Cook in double boiler over boiling water until thick. Cool and add whipped cream.

Sweet Dressing

1 cup (250 ml) salad oil
1 cup (250 ml) vinegar
½ cup (125 ml) maple syrup
½ teaspoon dry mustard

1 teaspoon paprika
1 clove garlic,
  sliced in half
1 onion, sliced

Combine all ingredients in a jar and shake well. Chill. Before using, remove the garlic and the onion.

Spiced Dressing

1 tablespoon chopped parsley
1 teaspoon chopped chives
½ teaspoon dry mustard
1 teaspoon salt
½ cup (125 ml) salad oil

¼ teaspoon pepper
2 tablespoons vinegar
1 teaspoon prepared
  horseradish sauce
1 scallion, finely chopped

Combine all ingredients and beat well. Chill.

Russian Dressing

1 cup (250 ml) mayonnaise
½ cup (125 ml) tomato sauce
½ cup (125 ml) chili sauce
2 tablespoons chopped chives
1 tablespoon minced parsley

1 hard-boiled egg, chopped
1 tablespoon lemon juice
2 tablespoons caviar
salt, pepper and cayenne
  to taste

Mix all ingredients together. Season to taste with salt, pepper and cayenne.

Chef's Salad Dressing

¼ lb (125 g) blue cheese
1 anchovy fillet, mashed
juice of ½ lemon
2 tablespoons vinegar

½ cup (125 ml) olive
  or salad oil
1 clove garlic, crushed
salt and pepper to taste

Crumble cheese. Add remaining ingredients and mix thoroughly.

Spiced French Dressing

1 teaspoon sugar
½ teaspoon salt
½ teaspoon dry mustard
½ teaspoon paprika
pinch of cayenne
2 tablespoons lemon juice
2 tablespoons vinegar

½ cup (125 ml) salad oil
½ cup (125 ml) chili sauce
½ green pepper, sliced
¼ onion, sliced
½ teaspoon oregano
½ garlic clove

Place all ingredients into an electric blender and mix for one minute.

Vinaigrette Dressing

½ cup (125 ml) olive oil
4 tablespoons tarragon vinegar
1 hard-boiled egg, riced

2 teaspoons finely chopped chives
1 tablespoon chopped parsley
salt, pepper and paprika

Blend oil and vinegar. Add remaining ingredients and mix well. Chill before serving.

Oil and Vinegar Dressing

1 teaspoon salt
½ teaspoon sugar
¼ teaspoon black pepper
½ teaspoon paprika

½ teaspoon dry mustard
1 cup (250 ml) salad oil
½ cup (125 ml) vinegar

Combine all ingredients in a jar and shake well.

Cooked Russian Dressing

¼ cup sugar
3 tablespoons water
½ teaspoon salt
½ teaspoon paprika
juice of one lemon

1 tablespoon vinegar
½ cup (125 ml) tomato sauce
1 tablespoon Worcestershire sauce
1 cup (250 ml) salad oil
½ onion, grated

Cook sugar and water until sugar is completely dissolved. Cool. Combine remaining ingredients. Add syrup and beat thoroughly. Chill.

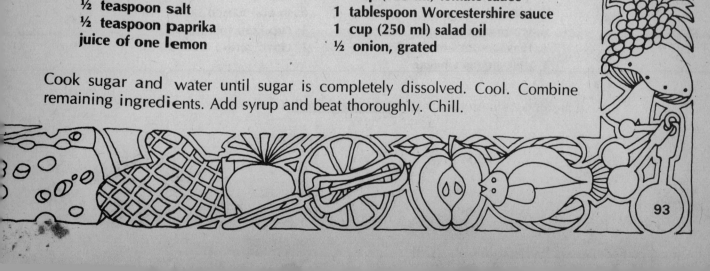

Mayonnaise and Chili Dressing

½ cup (125 ml) mayonnaise
½ cup (125 ml) cream
3 tablespoons chili sauce
juice of half lemon
1 tablespoon chives, chopped

1 teaspoon salt
pinch paprika and cayenne
1 tablespoon Worcestershire
sauce

Combine all ingredients and mix until well blended.

French Dressing

1 cup (250 ml) olive
  or salad oil
¼ cup (62.5 ml) vinegar
1 teaspoon salt
1 teaspoon sugar
¼ teaspoon dried basil
1 clove garlic, cut
  in half

1 teaspoon paprika
½ teaspoon dry mustard
1 tablespoon grated onion
1 tablespoon Worcestershire
sauce

Put all ingredients into a jar and shake thoroughly. Remove garlic before using the dressing.

Garlic Dressing

1 teaspoon salt
½ teaspoon pepper
¼ teaspoon cayenne
¼ teaspoon dry mustard
2 tablespoons vinegar

2 tablespoons tomato sauce
dash of Tabasco sauce
1 cup (250 ml) salad oil
1 clove garlic, crushed

Combine all ingredients together. Beat well. Chill.

Index